My Folly

by Carmela Maria

Preface

Many of my friends have asked me to write the story of my life. For over 30 years, different people have suggested that I write "This Adventure". Finally, with the help of several friends, we have printed this book...

"When I said 'Yes', it was God's yes, not man's. Agape (God's love) From the beginning God's love continues to grow concretely in my heart and in my life. Otherwise, this would be just a foolish love story, rather than a testament of God's power."

Acknowledgement

Thanks to all these people this book
has been able to be printed.
I extend my deepest gratitude to
each and every one of them.
Ella Dyer
Rachida
Nancy Ghaffari
Leethen Bartholomew
Roger Sonnati
Martine Hasdenteufel
Marie Fournier
Sylvia Cortese
Ninette Petruzziello
Marc Petruzziello

Table of Contents

Chapter

1 *A Bride is Born*

The year was 1997. When I arrived in Nice, France, to live in a senior citizen home, I knew no one and no one knew me. There have been many stories and movies about Americans living abroad, especially in Paris. This is my story.

This is not just a story about an American living in France; rather it is a story of a love affair, which has lasted for more than 58 years. It is a love affair with my husband, with his country and with a culture that is vastly different from my own. More importantly, it is a story of my unyielding faith in my Catholic beliefs. It is my story of the Lord Jesus Christ, my husband and me.

My grandfather had emigrated from Sicily, leaving Messine to find work. He went to South America after some agents had come to Sicily offering him a job. Once there, he realized that he was in a white slave camp from which he managed to escape. From his account we assumed that was in 1892 or 1893. He traveled all the way across Panama reaching New York and New Jersey, where he stayed because he found many Sicilians. He settled in the Italian colony and eventually his family joined him. First his wife arrived, and then his children followed.

My mother, Antonina La Monica, was 12 years old when she arrived in New Jersey to join her parents in about 1904. She worked in a pencil factory and could not go to school because the children made fun of the "ginny" green socks. That's how the fellow Americans used to speak of the Italians at that time.

The family, all seven children, arrived in the US via boat, after a month's journey. In 1905 a 26-year-old man left his family in Monreale, near Palermo, Sicily to go to New Jersey. First, he rented a room in my aunt's home, where he met my mother. Then his sister joined him and the rest of his family stayed in Monreale. Five years later, in 1910, they married. She was 18 and he was 31.

There is another Italian from the Hoboken area, more famous than I, Frances Albert or, as most people know him, Frank Sinatra. Like other immigrants, the Italians gathered together in areas similar to their homeland e.g. the Swedish in

Minnesota. Uncle Tony, my mother's brother, was a friend of Frank's at school. My family followed his career. Frank's first wife, Nancy, had their first child at Margaret Hague Maternity hospital in Jersey City where I was a student nurse.

My grandfather died in 1933. Although I was only eight years old, I remember that the funeral was a big event. There was a funeral procession, with music in the street and everyone wore black. My grandfather was part of a society, the Italian Club, which had a band. It was the first time I had seen a dead person. My uncle Danny said, "He went back home". Thus, it was not uncomfortable for me. To this day, when I see someone who has passed away I find comfort in my belief that his or her soul go home to God.

My paternal Grandmother and Grandfather.
From Monreale, Sicily

My maternal Grandmother and Grandfather.

We lived in Hoboken until I was 11 years old, it was an important part of my life. I was very happy and felt that everybody loved me. Most of the families in Hoboken had many children. It was a kind of community life. In those days we did not have much traffic so we used to often play in the street. Across the way from home was a large silk factory where we used to play a game that I loved the most. This game always had the same scenario; we had a king, a queen, princes, princesses, etc., and we changed roles so that everyone would have a chance to play the role he wanted. The stories were always beautiful, no violence, immorality or jealousy. We had not yet been exposed to any of these aspects of life via the movies or television. We were children, naive and pure.

From those games I believe I learned to visualize what heaven would be like. It helped me and still does, to accept the invisible world here and now, which is more real than the visible world that will disappear one day. The invisible world will last forever. I believe that our lives here on earth could be different if we really agreed with God's plan for us and obeyed and listened to him instead of to "our old nature" and the devil.

Each Friday when my father returned from work at 4:30 with his pay, he gave us a penny; the first thing we did was to go to the candy shop to buy a penny's worth of candies. What a treat that was! I still remember the anticipation of choosing the candies and the colors, and the smells of the shop. For one penny we could choose one chocolate in a big box, all of which had the same size and shapes. And, if one were lucky enough to choose a pink filling, you won another piece of chocolate.

My mother and father's wedding day

.

Me as a baby.

where I was born

We celebrated Halloween but it was very different from today. It was not with witches, and there was no treat or trick, nor horror, or violence. We used to play tricks on the trolley-car driver. I dressed like an old lady with a big shopping bag and a cane and would wait for the trolley to arrive. All the other children would hide. When the trolley driver saw me, he would come down to the curb to help me. As he approached me we would all begin to laugh and shout and run away. Poor trolley driver, please forgive us!

One of my favorite childhood stories (and one my

grandchildren have heard because they ask me to repeat it many, many times) involves make-up, mainly lipstick. I had a friend named Mary (unfortunately, I don't see her anymore) whose mother used to let her do almost anything she wanted to do; my mother was the opposite. My mother was very loving but we knew there were certain things we should not do.

One day, Mary and I found a tube of lipstick in the garbage can, which we used and we were thrilled. We felt very pretty and so grown up. My sister who was with us didn't put any on because she knew it was not right. We were too young to wear lipstick. I thought that my mom would never find out because we wiped off all the lipstick on my friend's slip. But my sister used it to blackmail me. She threatened to divulge the lipstick affair if I did not do the tasks mother requested. This went on for a few months, but it felt like a year, until one of my cousins who lived with us realized what was happening. She told my mother and I had to tell the truth about the lipstick. To my great surprise my mother laughed instead of scolding me. I was amazed and I was cured for life. From then on, I realized that honesty was the best policy and it has always been very important in my life.

My childhood was simple. Life was simple. Like many immigrants, we were living the American dream. We used to visit each other's families and at Christmas our gifts were simple: an orange or a banana. My father always did his best to give us a beautiful Christmas. I used to spend hours looking at the Christmas tree, mostly the crib underneath where the baby Jesus lay in the manger. We spent the entire month of December singing and listening to Christmas carols.

Despite the fact that we were living in a small apartment (a living-room, two small bedrooms and a kitchen for nine people) I have some very good memories, unlike my sisters, who were older than I. For example, our father bought a mechanical piano, which we had to pump with our feet; we used to play it all the time. Our family was very different from those around us. Many experienced fighting and jealousy, but we did not. My father was firm but loving and we would never think of talking back or being rude to either of our parents. I have a recent picture of this house, and along with the one next door, they are the only two homes, which still look the same today. The apartment was small and the kitchen also served as a bedroom. I had only one brother who slept on a cot, there.

Me standing in front of my birth
home in Hoboken 2008.

The first thing, I remember about Hoboken, was the bed in which I was born. Over the bed was a crucifix and in the dark it was fluorescent. I have always seen Jesus on the cross and this has been a very important part of my life. I was the only one in the neighborhood who had a big doll with real hair and a beautiful carriage. It was so precious to me that nobody was allowed to touch either of my cherished possessions. My sister Marion protected me from the children when I went out to play with my doll; she came with me. Unfortunately, this early guardian angel of mine died in 1987. I still feel as though she protects me.

We had many churches in Hoboken. The tradition for Holy Week was to visit three, six or nine churches where we adored the Blessed Sacrament on Holy

Thursday. My girlfriends and I tried to visit as many churches as we could, which we enjoyed. I no longer have contact with these friends who I enjoyed and who were mostly of Italian origin. Our lives went in separate directions after we were grown. I would like to know where they are today and how they are doing. My father had built a winepress and in September and October all the tenants in the house bought huge quantities of grapes and we made our own wine. It was very enjoyable to do this together; everything smelled of wine. My father filled his glass practically over the brim at mealtime and we would take turns having a sip. It is a pleasant memory.

I was nine years old the first time I went to the movies. By age 15, I had seen many films in which Charlie Chaplin, and Laurel and Hardy starred and Shirley Temple. I remember seeing an Alfred Hitchcock film. I was so frightened that from then on I was not interested in going to the movies again.

I was not exposed to anything I felt was not good for me. As the youngest in the family, I was not able to do as much as the others. I did only the shopping and the dishes, so when I married I had to learn how to cook and to look after my household. There was a hospital in the neighborhood where we used to go to weigh ourselves and I remember that my father was thrilled because at 11 years I weighed 100 pounds. He thought I was very healthy, as a result of his taking good care of his family.

Catholicism is very important to me because it is the foundation of our faith. I made my first communion at Our Lady of Grace's church in Hoboken. I remember so well the name of the Irish sister, Sister Eileen, who with clear and direct responses answered all of my questions about religion. Thank you Sister Eileen.

During that time we learned the catechism from a book with questions and answers we had to learn by heart. The first question is one I will never forget "Why did God create you?" And the answer was "God made me to know him, to love him, to serve him and to be happy with him, now and forever." That has stayed with me for all of my life. Another thing I learned by heart was the 10 Commandments; I realized that these commandments were simply rules of love, and if I did not obey them I would be unhappy. I knew that if I disobeyed my mother or father, I disobeyed God so it was very clear. It helped me to respect my parents.

(Photo of two sisters. Lily, Josie and me
when we received our first holy Communion)

Every Sunday, after mass we returned home
and my mother would quiz us about the gospel for
that day. I wanted to know all the answers, just
to be better than my older sisters in my mother's
eyes. I would listen attentively at mass, and
mother was always very happy with my answers!

There used to be a bread factory in Hoboken and
we were able to purchase the least expensive bread.
Bread was a staple in our meals and we were the first
people in the neighborhood to have a refrigerator.
Before having a refrigerator, we had to buy blocks
of ice from the ice peddler who passed through
the neighborhood. On Independence Day, July 4th

we had a huge fireworks show right in the middle of the street. It was beautiful I still remember my head resting on my mother's lap. She was sitting on the highest step of the house and I watched the fireworks. I had a feeling of security, being on her lap and in her arms, a warm memory, which is sparked every time I see fireworks. Actually, it was more of a hot memory because once a spark fell on my foot! The scar is no longer there but I remember it well.

I did not suffer from the lack of work and food, which others experienced. My sisters understood more about what was happening during that difficult time of the depression. The only memory I have about these hard times is that we were eating more bread, beans and soup than before. When we were sick, the doctor visited us. Whatever he prescribed he did so in large enough quantities for the entire family. At times it seemed like a real infirmary.

We had mountains of snow in the winter, which was fantastic for the children. We shoveled the snow on either side of the street; then we would slide down the high piles of snow. That was true sport.

We also had vegetable peddlers. Most of all I recall the trucks full of big watermelons. They always used to cut a wedge in the melon to show us the inside; if it was sweet, we bought it.

As the youngest child, I was well protected and did not have any of the problems my sisters experienced. At that time, in Hoboken, children began school at age six. My friends, siblings and most of the children on the street were older and away at school so I was very lonesome. I was only four years old, yet was admitted to kindergarten for two years.   No one recalls how such an exception was made. I imagine one of my parents, probably my mother, met with the principal since the school was less than a block away. I was allowed to attend school at an early age, and I had to remain in kindergarten until I was six. As I was rather talkative, the teacher would make me sit behind the piano and said that if I didn't remain quiet, she would cut out my tongue! That kept me quiet. Like the teacher, my mother kept a good watch on me as I was rather outgoing. Even at many social events like weddings and parties, my mother would call me back many times and make me sit by her!

Another fond memory is that of the many weddings that were held in our families. There were many varieties of sandwiches (ham, cheese, baloney and salami), dancing, and singing. Trays with Italian cookies, something I can still smell today, were plentiful during these celebrations. We used to call these "football weddings" because of the large rented hall and all the families working together as a team to make the sandwiches. Then, we sat on chairs around the big room in a circle, with space for walking around the group and dancing. My sister Sadie was the first to marry.

(Left to right above are my 6 siblings) Josey, Mama, Lily, Sadie my oldest sister as a bride, brother Mike, Ann, and Marion. 1943

Ann, Marion, Sadie, Josey, Lily and in front Mike & Mama around 1978 in the Fort Lee home bought in 1952. My picture on the player piano far left.

At the height of the depression we moved to Jersey City and out of our familiar Italian culture. This was completely different for us and I desperately wanted to fit in. I did not want people to know that I was Italian because so many of our neighbors were not. Our neighborhood included people of Irish, German and Jewish origin. I felt that I wanted to be like the others and unconsciously rejected my Italian background. We used to live in a large tenement house, an eight family home. However, when we moved to Jersey City we moved into a private home with a garden, bathroom, several bedrooms and a separate living room. It was a step out of the Italian culture into the American one. My father took out a mortgage and began to realize the American dream for all of us. We lived as though each day were Christmas. Every day was a feast. We were so happy to have a new house. For 14 days we were very happy. And, when my father returned from work the dream became even truer. It was like a party every night. He was thrilled to be providing all of this for his family. His dream was fulfilled.

At that time my father was an ironworker in a shipyard, the name of the company was Todd-Tietjen and Lang. Then, after those15 days, my father was killed in an accident at work. A distant relative who used to drink too much, had made a mistake with the valve of the boiler and my father tried to correct it, as he saw it was going to explode. Desperate to avoid such an accident and prevent further damage, he tried to adjust the valve. It exploded with such force that my father was decapitated. He was the only one hurt. It was September 14th, 1936, the Feast of the Holy Cross. He was 56 years old.

My mother was left with seven children. Despite this loss and the many difficulties following this tragic event she remained with us until her death in 1980, outliving my brother Michael by one year. She never remarried.

Our family has been blessed with longevity. Unfortunately, three of my sisters Sadie, Marion and Ann have gone home to the Lord. However, at the time of this writing some of my family members remain, Josephine and Lillian who live in New Jersey, not far from each other.

I attended both grammar school and high school in Jersey City. The most important memory I have after my father's death is that of my mother's health. My fear was she might die too so I prayed constantly that she be healed. She was in a kind of state of shock and depression for two years. A friend of the family, who had left the Catholic Church to become a member of the Pentecostal church, came to visit. Mother was between life and death. The friend prayed over her and she became well again. She felt she received a divine healing and became a Born Again Christian. She was then told that all of her children would need to become members of Pentecostal church or else they would go to hell.

In 1938 the requirements to become a member of Pentecostal church was to get rid of anything, which was linked to the former faith, in this case to the Catholic Church. This was very difficult for us because we had many signs of our faith throughout our home and we were asked to remove them all. Despite the difficulty of this request, it gave me the opportunity to try to understand why I wanted to remain a Catholic and what the church meant to me. I was thirteen years old and had just received my Confirmation. All I wanted to do was focus on my studies, my beliefs and the teachings of the church. My desire to learn was not fostered by the need to study with a priest or any other leader. Rather, I wanted to study on my own, examining the Catholic doctrines and faith and asking questions; this arose as a result of my desires.

The more I studied the more I realized I had no desire to change my religion. My mother became, and remained a fervent and obedient member of the Pentecostal church until the end of her life. She accepted the fact that my sisters were only lukewarm with regards to her new faith. However, it was more difficult for her to accept my brother's disturbance and confusion regarding her new faith. My father's untimely death changed our lives in more ways than many would have expected or have been able to foretell. My mother's decision to change her religion added to the impact this had upon our family.

She was only 44 years old when my father died and she never remarried. She was a disciple of Jesus and accepted what he preached. She loved him and prayed a lot. This gave her strength during this most difficult time and helped her live the remainder of her life in happiness and security despite her devastating loss. I became involved in many of the church activities: choir, bingo, and missionary work, just to name a few. I enjoyed the choir and missionary work the most. Bingo never really interested me. I was simply there to assist.

The owner of the shipyard where my father worked, helped us by giving my brother a job in the same facility where they taught him to work as a mechanic. Michael was nearly 18 and was like a father to us. My sisters Sadie, Ann and Marion went to work in the local sewing factory. Life began to resume some normalcy.

Because I was a good student, I graduated from grammar school at 14. I then went to high school, which was another big change for me. There were 5,000 students in the school and I began to mix with other cultures. I was part of the choir and I was very busy with many other activities in the school.

When I was about 12 years old, I had to go to the hospital for minor surgery. I stayed there for one week and when I saw the doctors and nurses at work I decided I wanted to become a nurse, I was driven to help other people. Another experience which marks my life was my mother allowing me to go out at night. Only once in a while would she do so but she would always remind me that I had to be home at a certain hour. I was in my teens and never once did I spend the night at a friend's house or anywhere else until I was 18 and went to nursing school.

One night she allowed me to go skating with my friend. We were so busy skating and having so much fun I forgot the time. When I came home it was late and all the lights were turned off. My mother was very kind and loving, so I did not fear her. I just went upstairs to the next door and there she was in the dark. She did not say a word; she just slapped me in the face. I realized that I had disobeyed her and in so doing I was disobeying God. I never did that again.

I have strived to be obedient and honest ever since I was very, very young. Both goals have served me well. I was a good student with good "marks" at school and my friends tried to copy my work. I would remind them that copying was the same as cheating and I wanted no part of it. If they wanted to cheat they were free to do so but without my help. They grew to respect me for my stance and I continued to learn that when you do things right you are much happier. Even the strictest teachers who wanted us to learn something the right way are the ones I remember most and appreciate the most..

At 18 years of age, I left home for the first time and entered nursing school. During those three years, I went to mass each morning in order to gain the courage to go to my classes. I would get up before everyone else, and since I was the first one awake, I would wake everyone else up when I returned from Mass. This was a community life.

When I left home to become a nurse it was almost like going to a convent. At that time in our school we lived in the spirit of Florence Nightingale. Our parents had never discussed sex and despite my studies to become a nurse, I had no idea what sex was all about. We did not even have sex education in school or during nurses' training. I seemed very different from my friends: more romantic about love and marriage. My friends began to talk about being in bed with men and making jokes about sex. I did not listen to or indulge in their conversations. But, one thing I knew from the age of 12 onward was that I was "in love" with someone. I do remember the first boy I was in love with; his name was Frankie. He never spoke a word to me nor I to him yet I was deeply in love with him without thinking of him on a sexual level. He was an alter boy. Just seeing him made me happy.

World War II increased in vehemence while I was almost finished with nursing school. I was preparing to help my country and the allies in our fight for freedom. I did not get the opportunity, as I finished my schooling in 1946, the war was coming to an end.

For years I remained in contact with many of the students I trained with. However, I have lost touch with most of them because many have died or moved elsewhere. The only person I still have contact with, one of my dearest friends, now lives in Canada. Before one could even get into nursing school one had to have a letter from a pastor, a letter from a teacher and, a letter from a friend. I remember the letter from the pastor, Father Schovlin in St. Ann's Parish in Jersey City. When writing my letter for school he said, "I am very surprised she wants to become a nurse, I always thought she would become a nun". That was very odd to me for I had never thought of becoming a nun. First and foremost, I wanted to get married and have a family. That was the ideal life for me.

When I left home I was very lucky to go to this nursing school. I missed my family very much, and of course, they missed me, the baby of the family. This school was like a home; we each had our own bedroom. Mine was on the 17th floor. It was called Murdock Hall and was my home for the next three years.

We would rise at 6:30 but it was very comfortable since you lived with the same students for three years. Our days were long, reporting for duty by 7:00 AM and allowed to go out at night until 10:00 PM, six days a week. Once a week we were allowed to sleep at home, we could go on Saturday night but had to return Sunday before 10:00 PM, fortunately the school was not far from my mother's home so I was able to visit weekly.

While in nursing school my family still lived in Jersey City, 87 Columbia Avenue. A few years later we sold that house and bought another one on Griffith Street, which was a three family house. When Sadie and Ann got married their families lived with my mother in this house. My mother had her own apartment in this house with my other sisters who were not yet married. Very quickly my brother married Viola and then Marion married and they were able to live in their own apartment in the same neighborhood. However, because I was the youngest and away at school I did not share this time of my family's life very much. Perhaps it was the beginning of my independence. My mother was living with Lily and Josephine "Josy" who were not yet married. Eventually, they married too and my mother lived with my sister Josy and her husband Tony. She was never alone thanks to this three-family home we had, and the community style life, with the privacy it offered even after marriage.

My sisters and me.

Chapter

2

A Daughter Lost

In 1952, almost at the same time that I met my husband; my family left Jersey City and bought another home in Fort Lee, New Jersey. This was another family home, large enough to house four families. My mother lived with Josey and Tony, my brother and his wife had their own private part of the home as did Sadie and Jimmy and Ann and Frank. It was a community life like a kibbutz. Only two of my sisters did not live in the family home but they did not live far away from it. Lilly lived just 10 minutes away and Marion remained in Jersey City, at that time only 30 minutes from my family's home. Everyone remained close in our family unit.

Once I graduated from nursing school, I began to work outside of New Jersey. I began to live my life and have many different experiences, some good and sadly, some very bad. With the exception of short visits I never returned to my family's home and unlike any of my sisters, I embarked on a life far from my family. I wanted to travel. I felt I needed to be far away from home. I had a desire to be different from those I loved, even though I loved and respected them very much. I just wanted to be me. I did not fit in, I did not think like them and I fear that they have suffered from these differences.

Yet, because of our family integrity, they were happy for me and encouraged me to pursue my nursing career and my desire to travel. That feeling and memory has always been very beautiful to me and many years later I realize how fortunate I was to have their love and support. That is why I have always returned albeit just for visits yet long enough to be with my loved ones.

New York 1952

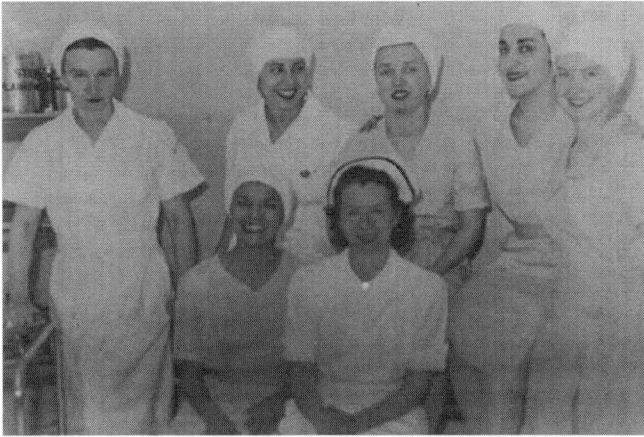

Second from the right is me, as an operating nurse.

In nursing school my dearest friend was more like a sister to me. We were all like family but Mary Mitchell and I were even closer than the rest. She did not have a family of her own so she really fit well into mine, like another sister. Today, we remain close even though she lives in Canada with her French Canadian husband and we don't write or see each other often. But, when we do it is as if we had just visited together only yesterday. We were opposites; I was the tall, fat one, and she was the petite, pretty one. I even had acne so the boys never looked at me only at her. However, I was not jealous. Her friendship was true, so nothing could foster hard feelings towards her within me.

One day she told me I had to lose weight because the boys would not look at me if I didn't. She suggested smoking, "…this way, you will not eat as much and you will slim down". I forced myself to start smoking at 19 and I became hooked. However, I never lost a pound or my appetite. I asked the directress of nurses about going on a diet. At that time additional precautions were taken before changing any regime. I was closely monitored and even x-rayed before receiving permission to change my diet.

For two years I ate no bread, sugar or potatoes. I only ate red meat and green vegetables. Gradually, I slimmed down so much so that by the time training ended, the directress said "…we cannot leave you like this; we have to get you a new outfit". I had to change all of my clothes and after that I never gained weight again, I learned a new way of eating thanks to my friend, who although her suggestion was not the ultimate solution, it had given me the idea. That is a true friend.

I lived in Murdock Hall during my training and worked for three months in Margaret Hague Maternity Hospital. During this time I began to date. I went with my friends to New York, meeting boys at bars and socializing in the evenings.

We visited Washington DC with "boyfriends" and even went on vacation to the shore or by the sea with others. We learned to flirt well enough to be invited and treated to dinner. However, I look back at that as the "shameful" part of my life and I am less than proud of such actions.

The end of our training coincided with the end of World War II. We had the offer to complete our training in either the Navy or the Army. The first 10 students, with the best marks were chosen. My friend and I were in this group. We spent the last six months of our training at Fort Dix Military Camp in New Jersey with the soldiers who had returned wounded from the War. We were called "Cadet" nurses with a special uniform.

Me as a "Cadet" nurse

Me with one of my best friends, Mitchell at Fort Dix

This was an excellent experience for us and after graduation I stayed a short time in Jersey City Medical Center but I always had the desire to travel. I wanted to travel and at that time, much like now, a nurse was able to travel and find work whenever she wished. I first wanted to go to California. My friend Mary and I wanted to go together but at the last minute, when everything was ready, she decided to stay because someone in her family was ill. Still desiring to travel I choose to leave Jersey City but for a closer destination, Washington DC. So I left by myself. This proved to be one of the craziest times of my life and, I only stayed six weeks! I worked in the hospital there but it was less than what I expected because I was very lonely without my friends and family. A glance through the local paper gave me additional incentive. The ad read, "For those wishing to travel, call this number".

This organization sold books and you traveled in a bus with a group, from state to state selling subscriptions and books. I decided to change my life so I left DC and traveled with this organization selling reading materials, mostly magazines. I don't recall any particular subjects but I found it interesting.

Within a month we arrived in Atlanta, Georgia in time for me to realize I had had enough and had made a mistake. I was not cut out for that career. Why? I was suffering from solitude. There was no recreation. You are out all day selling on your own and come home to sleep alone in a hotel room. People were just out to earn money. So, I called my family and told them I had decided to return home and continue my nursing career. Unfortunately, the experience was rather negative but it did reaffirm my desire to be a nurse, much like my religious experience earlier.

Returning to New Jersey was short lived as I soon found a good job in New York. My friend and I specialized in operating room procedures so we found jobs at Montefiore Hospital in the Bronx.

Another experience in my life and one crazier and more daring than any before was when one of our friends was leaving on a cruise and she invited us to a party on a boat. After it was time to leave we decided to stay on the boat. Mary Gonzales and I stowed away successfully until the boat passed the Hudson River and entered the ocean. There, headed for the wide expanse of the open sea the "control" was put into place. Of course, we did not have the proper papers and our lame responses were simply "we didn't realize, (we said we were drunk, which was not true) and we forgot". The ship's security was furious with us. They stopped the boat and a tugboat had to take us back to port. We climbed down the ladder to the tugboat, using large floodlights, as it was nighttime. We were guilty of being naive and innocent but having fun just the same. I enjoyed life and we found good jobs. Then, after a number of years my dear friend Mary married and moved to Canada. I continued to work at Montefiore Hospital. When Mary left it was as if my heart went with her. I seemed to have more fun being part of this duo especially as I searched for what I truly wanted, marriage and a family. On my own, away from my family and with my dearest friend gone, I met men who wanted only sex, something I realized I needed; ... And thought it would lead to my dream of marriage and family.

During this time the Huxley Report was published. A married roommate of mine was having an affair with a doctor who was also married. She was inclined to share her "wonderful" experiences with me. Naive people are easy to influence. Her talk of these beautiful experiences stimulated me in this yet unexposed part of my life. Unfortunately, many of the men were not interested in more than the proverbial "one night stand". Again, being naive and innocent, I did not understand nor grasp the consequences of such actions. Soon, I became pregnant. The thoughts of my family knowing about my actions made life unbearable. With my friend's help I found, what I thought was a solution: someone to perform an abortion. However, this solution was not a good one as I later learned. Unfortunately, no one around me told me I could have the baby, put it up for adoption or even keep it.

Sadly, I thought mostly everybody would have rejected me. Perhaps I asked the wrong people, perhaps I made yet another mistake by not asking my family, perhaps it was just too difficult at that time because we had not discussed sex and I was too ashamed to let my family know I had had sexual relations before marriage. Life was a very different time in those days.

After this most difficult experience, my resolve to travel by means of my nursing career was stronger than ever. I sought a position with the Navy because of its many benefits including full retirement after 20 years of service. I felt I had everything figured out so I went to apply, take the exams, received the initial "okay" and fulfilled my dreams. Again, another dream was not to be.

Between the first okay and the time I was to be inducted I went to the infirmary because of a bad cold. During a thorough check up urine analyses showed a problem with one of my kidneys. One had "dropped" and was no longer where it was supposed to be due to my weight loss. For the next year, in order to try to avoid surgery, I had to wear a special belt which was heavy and uncomfortable to try to keep the kidney in place.

Then the time to be inducted into the Navy came, so I said goodbye to everyone at the hospital and enjoyed a big going away party with many gifts. I was so proud to be going into the Navy and following my dreams.

Upon reporting to the Navy, with my health records, complete with x-rays, I found out I was to spend the next three days under supervision. The doctors were baffled. Had this been discovered while I was in the Navy I would have been operated on and may have completed my Navy career. However, since this happened between the days I was accepted and the day I was inducted, the Navy assumed no responsibility for me. I was in limbo. I was instructed to return to work, have the operation and come back. I was put on "reserved status". After the operation, I had to stay flat on my back for one month, without getting up for any reason. This was followed by six months of further convalescence and from then on I had to be very careful, not to lift anything heavy.

At this point I decided to go to France and work in the American hospital in Neuilly, near Paris. My application was accepted. There was just one thing I had to do before arriving in France. I had to learn to speak this beautiful language, which I did later, the hard way.

Chapter

3 *A Husband Found*

eanwhile, many miles across the vast Atlantic Ocean, in 1929, my husband was born, on the 22nd of December, in a small city of France. His father was a journalist and his mother traveled to many places with her husband. His father was a close friend of his mother's brother. His parents lived in Paris, the 16th section, but came to this small town because his grandfather was a country doctor and who had chosen to deliver him.

Everyone was thrilled at his birth! His grandmother and two aunts felt blessed .Yet, the only one who wasn't happy was his father. He did not like children and his mother suffered much at this occasion.

Later, they returned to Paris where my husband continued to grow. He never had a good relationship with his father. His father divorced his mother later on when he was young.

For all of his vacations, his mother sent him to the center of France, to be with his grandmother because of his poor health. When he was about 10 years-old, World War II broke out. He was placed in a boarding school in the center of France so he could be fed and continue his studies. Paris was occupied by the Germans so it was very difficult to find sufficient food and safety. He was very unhappy for all those years away from his family.

After the war, when he was about 15 or 16, he continued his studies in another part of France near the mountain region of the Alps not far from Switzerland. He completed his studies and passed his Baccalaureate, a diploma equivalent to two years of American college. He had good friends and enjoyed skiing and other winter sports. Here, at last, he was very happy.

Around this time he became, as he called himself, an atheist and started to have different immoral experiences. He had a great desire to travel and become a journalist, like his father, with whom he had very little or no relationship and who would never even helped him find a job! As a young man he spent a short time in Israel and enjoyed living in a Kibbutz; a special kind of community life.

When he was 22 he left France on a special assignment. He was sent out by a Paris company, with an older journalist, to spend two years in New York working on a French American newspaper. It was published for the French Embassy, for the French colony in this part of the States. This position was extremely important for him as a test to determine whether he would be employed by the company or not.

His father at this time was a famous journalist and director of a magazine in Paris. He lived six months of the year in New York and six months in Paris between the times that he traveled all over the world. So it was at this time that he started to develop a new relationship with his father. His father was proud to see that he was very talented!

In 1952, after years of independence, I married for the first and final time. How did I meet my husband?

One day my friend Marie Gonzales met a young French man in a French restaurant where she often went with her boyfriend. Since my heart was broken from my last relationship, I had no interest in dating but my only motivation to accept this invitation was to learn to speak French. This is the reason why I accepted and met my future husband for the first time between Christmas and New Years of 1951. "This was not love at first sight," This was not my type of man! He was blonde, shy, and not very tall. I loved men who were tall, dark and handsome!! After this first meeting, he invited me for dinner and at a New Year's Eve party in the same restaurant called Jean du Midi. We started off with a drink, followed by a good French dinner and then we danced all night. After we left the restaurant, we were standing on Times Square, 42nd Street. I looked at the clock and I said to my future husband, "Oh I have to go to mass and I have to go to work at 7 am, bye, bye. I will call you tonight" He was perplexed! He thought I would go back to his room and instead I just left him flat, and left to go to mass! He was amazed! How could a girl do that? It shocked him!

It was hard for us to communicate because he spoke very little English and I spoke no French but every time we met which was every night, we made progress. What I appreciated most in him was his maturity for such a young man. He was 22 years old, very direct, very sincere, truthful, respectful and transparent. About the middle of February 1952, he asked me to marry him and knowing that if I said yes, a year later we would have to go to France to live there. After the proposal he suggested that we don't see or speak to each other for a week, so I will have time to think things over. If I said 'Yes', we would start to live together and prepare legal documents to be married at City Hall and later in the Catholic

Church. We were sure of what we wanted and what was essential for each of us. So he promised me that he would never hinder me from practicing my faith and having our future children baptized. Besides that, he was happy to marry a woman who had conviction. As for me, I promised him to never talk to him about God and to never pray in his presence, as my future husband at that time was an atheist. During that week I had no idea what to do.

No one could help me to make this decision except God. So everyday after work, I would spend hours at church asking God to give me insight to know what to do. God then spoke to me "in my heart" and he showed me the life I had lived, my sins, my desires, my needs and all different things etc.

At the end of the week, I had a peaceful conviction that I should say 'yes' to God and to my fiance. We immediately lived together and probably conceived our first and only son on February 20th 1952. We found a furnished studio apartment and waited for the official documents to come from France. At that time in 1952 the mail between the USA and France was extremely slow. Finally, we got married on the 21st of March 1952 at City Hall and received benediction of our marriage on the 19th of April 1952. It was celebrated by a French priest in both French and English, at St. Vincent De Paul, a Catholic church in the Village section of New York City. Our ceremony was very simple, no white dress and no photographers. We did not have much money and my future husband was timid and he did not like big receptions. Besides that, we had to save our money to be able to go to France the next year. We had dinner at Jean Du Midi with about eight of his coworkers from France and USA. Even his father's secretary was there!

Our son was born on the 20th of October 1952 and we left the United States for a journey through life, much like that of Abraham, who just trusted God and traveled into the unknown.

We arrived in Paris on February 14th, 1953, which is St. Valentine's Day. This day for lovers is based on the French tale of the imprisoned saint. Perhaps it was an omen and although I have not felt imprisoned, I have felt completely united to my adopted country.

For the next five years, we lived in Paris in the 16th section. Then, we left the big city for the country and the myriad of new experiences for which that lifestyle had to offer. As a journalist my husband and I traveled throughout Europe seeing first hand the rebuilding of cities and entire countries in this post war era. My husband's task was to document this work as well as other varied subjects such as the arts, in England, Spain, Belgium, and Switzerland and of course, all throughout France.

By 1959, we bought our first home in the center of France where we would go on weekends, every fifteen days for two years. It was a house without comfort and in 1961 we left the Parisian area and settled there, only visiting the US once in about a dozen years. In our new home we experienced another way of living, among the peasants and farmers of this rural area.

We hired a man who came every day to the house to take care of the garden and the properties. For my son's 10th birthday, my American family sent us some money to buy a donkey for him.

When this man and I went to the nearby farm to buy the donkey, we had to cross over a wooden bridge to get to our home. One rainy afternoon, in October or November, it was already dark and the donkey was scared and stubbornly refused to cross the bridge. One of us had to stay with the frightened animal while the other went back to the other farms to find four men who carried her over the bridge. We tried to train her but after that incident, and many more, we realized she had trained us. Her name was Penelope and she became a part of our family. Our son was so thrilled to have her and he dreamed of taking care of her but on the first day of grooming the donkey, she kicked him and he lost the passion that he had of taking care of her. She may have been stubborn but she also had a good heart. When I had problems, I felt I could go to the stable or the field and speak my mind. She seemed to listen, especially when I cried. For ten years I never even talked about my faith.

A few years later my husband converted to my faith. He had been to a funeral mass of one of his professors from boarding school and during this mass he regained his faith in God. Suddenly he was touched by grace. All of his former Catholic faith was renewed and he was converted.

During the first 10 years of our marriage, I never spoke of God to my husband. I never bothered him with my spiritual life. I respected what we had promised each other before our marriage, the promise that he would never stop me from practicing my faith and that we would raise our children in the church. I promised never to speak about God or pray before my husband. So, it was a shock to me when he returned to our faith.

It was because of rediscovering his faith that

he felt a need to speak to a Priest who he had known for a long time that knew him very well and discuss what happened to him and what to do next. However, the priest did not know what to tell him. He wanted to go further so he immediately found an organization in a parish to help the poor. He wanted to find a priest he had known when he was a young man but had no success.

One Sunday morning, instead of going to our Parish for mass, about eight kilometers from our home, the Parish Priest was saying mass in another village. A lady came up to us and asked whom we were. She said there was a Priest in her home recovering from an accident, and he was looking for us. He was a member of the Charles de Foucauld family and we were happy to have found him.

Thanks to this priest we went to Paris where we became involved with the fraternity in our home. A fraternity is a small group of lay Catholics and a priest; all who want to live the Charles de Foucauld spirituality, a more radical and evangelical calling. Charles de Foucauld was beatified on November 13th, 2005; his feast day is the 1st of December, the day he was assassinated in his hermitage in the desert in 1916. These groups in different parts of France meet once a month for the whole day for fellowship, prayer, adoration and meditation on the Bible. Daily at their home, they read the Bible at least 15 minutes or more, prayed to the Holy Spirit three times a day, enjoyed daily mass if possible and adoration of the Blessed Sacrament in their own churches. They welcomed all people of any background or religion, especially the poor. It is," The Universal Brotherhood", like Charles de Foucauld. There are many priests, nuns and other followers of Charles de Foucauld in different congregations throughout the world who remain faithful to his teachings. Anyone wanting to know more must simply contact the Little Brothers of Jesus or the Little Sisters of Jesus.

After praying together for two years we were finally able to find 8-10 people for our fraternity.

One day we made contact with gypsies. Never before had we heard of them nor were we even aware of their culture. They had problems in France and Europe especially during the war when they, like the Jews, the handicapped, homosexuals and Jehovah's Witnesses, were victims of the Nazis.

When an elderly woman came with a little boy, her grandson, she had beautiful baskets to sell so we invited her in, we talked, had some coffee and then she left. From that day forward our home was never without the visit of gypsies. In our home they found a place where people were not afraid of them. We became very involved and eventually too many gypsies came to our home. We tried to help them financially and to find work and to pass their driver's test, etc., all necessary to become independent citizens of France.

A priest, who was in the fraternity with us, met an assistant social worker that was also a nun. Through her we found that there were eight families like us who were helping the same gypsies in different sections of our diocese. We had all reached the point that we did not know what more we could do. We met each other and pooled our resources in order to help the gypsies. We went to see the Bishop and indicated that we needed assistance on behalf of the gypsies. We did not have a priest available at that time so each month we organized a meeting in a different parish. While waiting for a priest, he sent us out with his blessing as a "Ministry for Gypsies to Evangelize".

In these different parishes we first had to convince the priest not to be afraid of the gypsies and then we had to organize a mass and a meal together with the parishioners and the gypsies. This was something very new and good because when this group went in different parishes teachers, other social workers and even the police came in and helped, trying to get to know these people and better understand them.

Due to these meetings in different parishes a new group was started by a Lay Association to benefit the gypsies. This addition completed the religious ministry; most of us were part of both. We were not alone anymore and it was very rewarding for all of us, especially the gypsies.

In 1965, we received another blessing. It was the gift of our youngest son, who was born in 1963. During all our years of marriage my husband and I wanted more children. We always wanted a large family; my husband wanted eight boys and I wanted daughters as well. However, I couldn't get pregnant again and at that time it was very hard to adopt a child in France.

So, we sought out an "assistance public", a social worker, in order to become foster parents. We told her that we had a lot of love to give to a child as well as a home and money. We asked the social worker to help us with the intention of keeping the child for an extended period of time. During that time, they made many inquiries both concerning our home and us. Then, six-months later while my husband was in his office, we received a telephone call from the assistant social worker. She inquired of us, if we still wanted a child. Our answer was of course positive.

The following day she brought us our second son.

Before his arrival, we had no idea if we were going to adopt a boy or a girl. We had nothing ready, no baby bed, food, nothing. We were completely unprepared. We were very excited and asked friends to lend us a crib, clothes and other things an infant needs.

The next day a small car arrived in the courtyard of our home with the assistant social worker and a little boy, who looked like an angel. He had been born to a woman who was unable to care for him and left him after two months. He was 22 months old when he came to our home, to our family.

We did not want to know too much about his background because we did not want to lie to him if he ever asked us about his origins.

When our youngest son arrived, we were leaving for Easter vacation, so we took him with us to Paris. When we returned we had to make some adjustments. For example, we spoke English but my youngest son only knew French. Like us, everyone fell in love with our new son. There was only one thing some may have considered less than perfect about our youngest son, his ears, which were a bit prominent.

Our youngest son and the gypsies came into our life about the same time. Our home was,"la maison du bon Dieu", the home of the good God.

We were the ideal family, a lovely couple and every thing was perfect. We had enough money and friends and our home was open to everyone. Even the Bishop allowed us to have the Blessed Sacrament in a chapel in our home. Later we had a priest full time to help us with the gypsies. This priest slept once a week at our home. It was a very spiritual life, very busy but in great peace; we kept our life simple. Anyone could come at any time to our home. We never knew how many people were eating at our place either during lunch or dinner.

We had a vegetable garden so it was easier to make a large pot of soup. My husband had just left his job as a journalist to become a writer so he was home working during the day. At night anybody could come to our home to join in fellowship but they had to either eat before or after because all we proposed was a bowl of milk, from our neighbor's farm, coffee or chocolate, bread, butter and jam, and everyone had to wash his or her own dishes.

We had to simplify things because I could not handle two meals a day and my husband had to work so he could not help me; he was doing his work and I was doing mine. I never felt that I was my husband's slave because he did not help me. Many women would have found such a life very difficult. However, I never had a problem especially due to the love and support of my husband's family. Like the women in his family, I enjoyed serving men, and didn't feel nor share the opinions of some modern women that it was a life of domestic slavery.

In 1968 – 1969, we began hearing about the hippie movement in America. My husband decided to investigate this movement in the United States for his magazine and perhaps write a book. His work was a very important part of our life so we left France to visit my family in New Jersey. To begin this research we bought a used car and went to California. There was another woman who was also interested in writing a book so she traveled often with my husband. I did not travel with him all the time because of some of his destinations. He went to what was known as drug camps, met Timothy Leary, and researched the culture of the hippy community. My husband wanted this experience first hand in order to write a book. When he returned to France he wrote a book. He read chapter by chapter to me as he did with his articles.

When the book was published, he read it to our oldest son who was about 17 at the time. I started to feel very uncomfortable with this book (and did not know why my husband had such a fascination with it) and the way he presented it bothered me. However, I didn't understand why.

To me it seemed that maybe this book inspired my son to leave home to be "free" like the hippies. But, he was also having problems at school and since he was no longer working, we agreed to give him his freedom, only if he passed the baccalaureate degree. We paid a large sum of money for a summer school program in order for him to pass his exams. He left home at 18.

We wanted to help him financially, but he did not want us to do that. We felt as though the umbilical cord was cut. We were able to let go the right way because we knew that as parents we had tried our best. We had made a lot of mistakes and we asked God to forgive us.

We wanted to free our son but he knew that he could come back home at any time. He could call us at any time; our hearts and our doors were always open. He left and we saw him only once in a while when he came back to our home, but he was not the same. His hair was longer and we saw that he was becoming addicted to drugs. No questions were asked. We went on with our lives. We felt blessed and were very happy raising our younger son and continuing our work. Then, our dream became a nightmare. It was as if we had suffered a terrorist attack, like that of 9/11.

Up to this point, in 1971, despite many changes, everything was fine. Our oldest son had left, our youngest was eight years old and we were still very involved with the Gypsies. One day one of our friends, who ran a restaurant not far from home, met a couple that bought a house about 5 or 6 hundred meters from our house where they visited annually. This time they came for a month to renovate their home. They were from Marseille so a friend of ours introduced us to the family, a husband and wife (they had been married for 25 years, with two grown children and two younger ones, a boy and a girl).

They were a very nice family, working hard on their home, doing much of the work themselves. Being neighborly we invited them to bring their lunch and eat with us almost daily. After lunch, which was outside next to a bubbling brook, they would return to their home and their work.

Fifteen days later my husband and this woman were together.

Chapter

4 *Faith Renewed*

I realized that they were extemely attracted to each other, but I did not know exactly what was going on, or how serious it was. After this woman and her husband returned to Marseille, my husband told me about his feelings for her. I was in shock! This was worse than the first shock, which I had experienced 10 years before.

During that time we lived in the country about 50 kilometers from Paris in a hamlet, without any facilities and here I learnt a new way of living, so different from my own. The people who lived in this hamlet were very kind, simple, humble and hard workers in the field and we became a part of this living. We originally moved there because my husband loved the country. I loved the city, and was never exposed to the mountains. I had never even seen a cow. Being in nature for me meant being at the beautiful Jersey Shore with sand and sea. I loved high heels and Elizabeth Arden! Now I was living something extremely different in the country. We had no running water and no heat. We had just one fireplace that needed wood to work. We had no toilets, just a pail in the back yard in a little cabin. In the kitchen, we cooked with coal.

My husband worked in Paris and he came home every night. One day he came home and told me that he was going to leave me because he met a very beautiful model that fell in love with him. So he left, I was in a state of shock, during 3 days and 3 nights I neither ate nor slept, just turning pages of my Bible hardly reading anything. After these 3 days, very calmly I decided that now I am only 36 years old, I would leave with my son, return to the USA and continue my nursing career. So to let my French family know what had happened and what I planned to do, I left by train with my son to visit my husband's aunt and uncle's home where we enjoyed going very often. While we were eating with them and their parish priest who we knew very well, I told them the entire story and how I was so sorry for my husband, who had never received love from his father, who had divorced his mother, and besides that my husband was an atheist etc. The only thing I could feel for him was a deep compassion, for he never experienced what I was blessed with all the love of my parents and my faith. After all that I told them about my plans to return to the United States. The next day I went to confession to this priest, who was present at this dinner. The priest told me, "Carmela don't leave for the United States, stay home and wait for your husband to come back because the love you have for him is *1 Corinthian 13 verse 4 – 8.*" (*Love is patient and kind; Love is not jealous or boastful: It is not arrogant or rude. Love does not insist on its own way. It is not irritable or resentful, It does not rejoice at wrong ,but rejoices in right . Love bears all things, believes all things, endures all things. Love never ends.*)

What the priest had told me about not leaving for the United States, to stay home and wait for my husband to come back, was like God himself telling me these words in my heart. So, I decided to do what he said, and I received a great peace and never came back on this decision. During 6 months my husband visited with his girlfriend, they ate with us and we took long walks together in the country etc. I didn't suffer at all from these visits, I stayed in total peace, and resting on these words,' wait for your husband and don't go back to America."

About the end of these 6 months, one day my husband came alone, completely disgusted and confused. When I asked him what was wrong, he told me 'don't ever speak to me about women. I asked my boss to send me to Madrid, the furthest place possible and the longest time possible.' The reason for this new situation was that he had gone to see a lawyer to find out how he could divorce me. At this time in France it was not easy to get a divorce. When he heard all the horrible things and lies he had to do and say against me, this disgusted him completely. He said good-bye and he left for Spain.

About 15 days later, he called and told me to take the train and join him in Madrid. We never came back and talked about the past. Our love grew even stronger because of this trial.

Therefore, due to this previous experience I had hope. I hoped this new situation with this new woman would also be over quickly. The only thing that helped me not loose my mind was God who gave me words of life. Daily, I repeated these words and have continued to do so since 1971:

Hope against all hope", "*Man cannot separate those that God has united*", "*Did not I tell you; if you believe you will see the glory of God and forgive 70 times seven.*"

That was all I could think of. Both couples never thought that this could have happened to us. No one in our fraternity group knew what was going on except us so we discretely tried to find some help. We knew that if we involved our small fraternity group or our family, it would have been even more difficult.

Only three priests knew about our situation. One of the priests told my husband to follow the light he was receiving. Ten years later I met that priest again in Ireland, where I was selling tapes at a large, very charismatic, international conference. When the two of us were alone I told him that I had a hard time forgiving him for how he had directed my husband but now, I was relieved to ask him to forgive me. We continued talking until we had no more to say. A short time later he came back and said, "You know Carmela, it is my turn to ask you to forgive me because on the day your husband came to see me, I was in a horrible situation with a woman and I just could not tell him the truth because I was living something as difficult as he was living." The chaplain who was working with us in our ministry for the gypsies was my only personal support, thanks to him I was able to live in trust and love with everyone for nearly two years. The four of us tried to find a way to come back to being individual couples and stay friends, which meant that for a certain period my husband lived fifteen days with this other woman and fifteen days with me. During the times he was with her I was on my knees in the chapel, praying, "I want to forgive them, I want to stay in my marriage". God gave me the grace to do so. When my husband came home I treated him as my husband. It was not smooth all the time, there were arguments, and finally the other woman's husband lost his job and had a nervous breakdown. They had no money so we tried to help them. They left Marseille and we tried to live a kind of community life together. When we had this idea, for them to leave Marseille permanently and live near us, it was the final hope because we sincerely felt we had tried everything.

They all thought, except me, that everyone would just live in the same house and that we would all be good friends. Immediately, when they arrived with their two children, I explained to them that this was not my way to live. But, that they should live in their house we would live in ours and we would have meals together daily, one day at their home and the next at ours and that we were going to share our wealth with them. Once we began this way of life my husband and the other woman did not have to leave as often. Rather, they began to be together just one weekend every fifteen days, then one weekend a month. To me this seemed as though we were getting close to the end of this difficult time. My husband was thrilled and so was I for we could see that we were finding a solution, my husband was returning to me completely and the other woman was returning to her husband.

Yet, the other woman could not handle this, she could not let go of my husband and tried to stop everything, that was early September in 1972. She left France to visit her son who was in Israel in the army. My husband took me on a trip for his work where he was beginning a book on community life in France. The oldest community that existed in France, Community of L'Arche, a non violent community founded by Lanza del Vaso, where we visited often to learn how to live a more simple life. There were people from all different religions who lived together and respected each other and remained faithful to their own religion, they even had a common prayer. There was no confusion rather it was a beautiful community.

We spent one week with them and while I was there I asked a companion for advice. I was advised to come to a prayer meeting. I had no idea what that was but I went to this group. I saw these people praying yet they had no answers for my problems but I went to two meetings during that week. Then on the last night, which was the feast day of Saint Michael, Saint Gabriel and Saint Raphael the archangels and also the feast day of the community, we had a large party even though this simple life had no gas or electricity. Yet, we had a wonderful time. It was September 29 1972, and at this feast day and party, which started with about 100 people all together in a large beautiful room, we prayed together. As soon as I heard one voice praying, the Holy Spirit literally descended upon me. I trembled, screamed and cried. A few people who had been baptized in the spirit, laid hands on me and I was completely renewed and released, happy in the love and peace of God.

Later, people told me that I had been filled with the Holy Spirit. I did not stay for the rest of the evening because we had to leave to go back home which was 800 kilometers away.

At this time in France, in 1972, it was the very beginning of the outpouring of the Holy Spirit, which had started a few years before in the Catholic Church in America. I knew nothing about this and that it had happened in many parts of the world and in other Christian churches. The people who prayed with us told me that I had received many graces of God. I had no idea what that meant at that time. While walking up the mountain in the moonlight to join my husband who was already in bed, I sang in tongues.

The next morning, during our trip back home, my husband spent his time lamenting over his girlfriend who had left and how unhappy he was without her. All this seemed like I was no longer disturbed or unhappy. I was in a state of protection, peace, joy and love for Jesus. I thought of the hymn Amazing Grace, how sweet the sound.

We learned a lot from this community, how to spin wool, etc. it was a peaceful place to be, but we returned home, to the same hopeless situation with no solution. Previously, I used to cry often because I was so unhappy, however, now I was in a blessed state that lasted for a month or more and the Holy Spirit led me as if I was in a charismatic prayer group, which did not yet exist in this area.

When we returned I went to see the priest who was in charge of the gypsies. This went on for about a month. Then one day I told the priest that something was bothering me, something I did not understand. When I was in this community they told me that I had received many blessings. The priest said that if it were the Holy Spirit that I had received we would see it by its fruits. I needed this Holy Spirit because the hardest part of my life was coming.

The four of us couldn't go any further; the other woman spent the entire day at our home, working with my husband in his office and she returned to her home at night. I could no longer handle this. It was just too hard and there seemed to be no solution. I suggested that my husband leave with the other woman and I would stay in the house that I loved so much. My husband did not want to leave the house but it had become unbearable for him, to the point that for the first time he became violent. He began telling me that he would not give me any money to look after the house and that he would not help me financially. I resisted his threats but never sought a lawyer to protect me even though I had as much rights as he did to stay in our home. I refused any outside help.

My help came from the Lord.

My husband was going through torture, he had two women who would not let go of him and he was to the point of suicide. His pain gave me the courage to say I will leave. In my heart God gave me an image of Solomon who spoke to two women about their babies. One of the babies died during the night and the mother exchanged the baby. Later, both women said the live, healthy baby was theirs. Solomon said if you cannot decide whose baby it is I am going to cut the baby in half. The real mother said no. The same happened with me. I would rather have a husband who is alive even though I cannot live with him. I gave up my husband, and my home to save my husband, my marriage and to please God.

5 *The First Crossroad*

I began to look for a place to continue my life with my youngest son who was not officially adopted yet. I went to L'Arche community of Lando Del Vaso. There they told me that it would not be good, and that it was too difficult to stay there without my husband. In February, during the school vacation, I went to a community near Lyon called The Little Brothers and Sisters of the Gospel, in the spiritual family of Charles de Foucault. They found a place for me. In June 3rd of 1973 I left home after 20 years of marriage, with only what I could put in a trunk of a car.

After that, he drove me to a new place where I would live with my youngest son. Finally the sisters found a house for us and my youngest son went to a local school.

The house that
I lived in
was near the
Little Sisters of
Charles Foucauld.

My husband came every few months to see us. I thought I would be back home six-months later. But soon, I realized that was not going to be the case. I still lived in hope of going back home soon. After nine months we realized that I could not adapt to this new place and needed to go back to the center of France and continue my work, albeit part time, with the gypsies. This was not far from my home where my husband still lived with the other woman. This way, he could visit us.

Even my husband knew that the best thing for me was to go back to the center of France and continue my work. So he found a house for us to rent. Before leaving this area with all our plans everything was going well except my health. I became so weak I started getting dressed at 8:00 in the morning and was finally dressed by noon. I could not take any more medication. I could not have more faith or more hope than I already had. I was full of desire to live and not be so weak.

I went to see a priest and asked him to pray for me and to give me the sacrament for the sick. He placed his hands on me and I was filled by the Holy Spirit and healed divinely. That was January 25th, 1974 when I heard in my heart, "...you shall not die...you shall not die and you will live to publish the wonders of God". I was so filled with this spirit and healed that I continued for 13 years without any medication except an aspirin one time. My strength came back gradually, my arthritis and rheumatisms vanished and I became a new person.

By March of 1974 we were ready to go back to our new house about forty kilometers from our original home in the center of France. Its proximity allowed my husband to visit our son and me. We had decided this but when our youngest son heard that we were not going back home he cracked. He became violent and would cry "my school, my dad". It was heart breaking. I could not console him for he was rejecting me completely. If he could he would have killed me.

He started saying bizarre things to the neighbors, different stories about me. I realized we were at a crossroads; my son could run away trying to escape the turmoil and disappointment of his home life.

I called my husband. When he heard what was happening he was very concerned. We had only two solutions, my youngest son goes back to the public assistant or go live with my husband and the other woman and her two children. The other woman finally accepted this situation and my youngest son left with his father.

It was very difficult for me to let go of my youngest son but I had no choice and I remembered what the priest and others who had prayed for me had told me, it gave me great encouragement.

They said, "your youngest son cannot understand what you are doing for him right now. But when he can, when he is an adult and he understands such things he will be very close to you, his mother". Years later I learnt they were right.

Finally, I went to the center of France in this new house where I thought I would have a normal life and be happy with my son. In this home without my youngest son I decided to work with the gypsies full-time.

Although I did not know how it would work out I knew I had enough room to make a "fraternity" where others who share my faith in the Lord could come and live with me. We would be together in our shared faith and our shared home but separate, free to work in different ways. I tried for a year and a half, to no avail, to find the proper people for a fraternity. Unable to do so, I had no solution. Because I never make a decision on my own rather, I always seek spiritual counseling everyone was praying. We were trying to find people for our fraternity however, nothing worked. It came to a point where I had to decide. I saw what was happening when I returned home, well after 9:00 PM. It was very difficult especially during winter. I was tired after a day with the gypsies and other tasks. Plus it was too dangerous for me to come home by myself. The only solution was to find a camper and live with the Gypsies full time. This way I was no longer alone and I was no longer in danger while going back and forth to my empty and cold house. It was a crazy idea but there seemed to be no other solution. My spiritual counselor Sister Yvette, who was aware of my situation, suggested that I buy a camper and live with the gypsies? It was pure folly but I had no other solution. With the help of the gypsies, we found a small camper and I had just enough money in my bank account to purchase it. At the same time I kept the house I was living in so that in the summer my grandchildren could vacation with me. And this is the way I started a journey that lasted 10 years.

The gypsies and I are in front of my campers

Chapter

6 *Gypsy Life*

The Bishop gave me permission to have a chapel with the Blessed Sacrament in my camper. There, I prayed and read the Bible for long hours before opening my door to share my time with the people around me in many ways.

I traveled with the gypsies for about ten years in this camper. This was the "Manouche" tribe and they are not big travelers. They are people who stay in one area and go from camp to camp, about 200 families in all. Everybody wanted me to stay with their family so I would stay three months with one family and when they left the camp I would move with them. After three months with a family I would leave to spend a few weeks with my children and later on with my grandchildren. I would return to the Gypsies and continue my three-month per family stay. I shared their life and I was able to do so because most of the Gypsies used to come to our home as poor people who needed help. Now I was the poor person who needed help. They knew what I was experiencing at that time. It was very good for me as well as for them. No matter where we went I was a bridge between the non- gypsies and the gypsies.

By now, it was 1975 and I had never camped in my life. I had no idea what it was like to live in a camper. I was fifty years old. In that part of France, Gypsies could only stay in the campground reserved next to the garbage dump or the cemetery. There was no electricity or other facilities like the campgrounds that exist today. There were no trees, which was very difficult during the hot summers. Yet, I got through that challenging time.

The Gypsies and me '

When the first winter came I said my "God" how am I going to get through this? My camper was so small and I only had a small wood stove. So

we had a big fire outside to warm ourselves before going to bed even during the rain, and wind. I said if I can get through this alive it must mean that my place is here. That winter I lived through this extreme situation without even getting a cold yet everyone around me was sick. I knew I was blessed.

I shopped for my own food eating mainly fruits, vegetables, mostly raw carrots, cheese and an occasional piece of meat. I could not spend too much money because with the money my husband was giving me I had to pay for my car, insurance and gasoline. At that time we used Francs rather than Euros so I had the equivalent of about five Euros or $5.00 a day to spend. I got used to it.

It was a good experience for me to continue in this

new way of life. I loved not thinking about tomorrow but living only for the Lord and only for the day.

As I mentioned earlier, the Gypsies made baskets and every morning they would sell them so they would have food for the day. We were completely dependant on God and the generous people we meet which gave us a lot of freedom. Life in the camper was not too difficult; it was nice warming up once the sun came up. We did not have to bother getting dressed up. I learned to live sometimes with only three liters (less than a gallon) of water a day, to cook and wash yet we were as clean as anyone else. When we had to camp near the garbage dump sometimes the children would find toys or other beautiful things in the rubbish. They would go wild with glee over such treasures and it gave us great joy to share in their happiness. However, when the sun went down the rats would come out for anything we left outside. All was destroyed within minutes so we had to be very careful not to litter, which was a good habit for everyone.

These were some of the best years of my life. Yet, after 10 years I decided I was ready for a change despite knowing that I would miss my life in my caravan. One of the reasons I finally left my life with the Gypsies was because they gradually lost their identity. They became influenced more and more by our way of living and culture.

Before, children and older people used to spend time together at night playing games and talking, saying prayers, singing and dancing, etc. Once they had television all fellowship at night stopped and even earlier in the day.

I did not want to put a television in my camper. Therefore, I was more alone than before. The children used to love to spend time with me. The television fascinated them so much that everything we once did together, especially regarding God and religion, became secondary. I had no reason to stay. Our mission was evangelism and it was over. The Priest left before me.

The Little Sisters of Foucauld and the caravan

I used to pull my camper with my Volkswagen. In 1985, I found another house in the center of France where I lived for two years. At that time I used to go back to America in the winter for six months and spent the rest of the year in France. I was able to visit my family as well as a gypsy family in the USA.

During the winters I would visit my family in America because it was too expensive to heat the house with electric heating in France and it was a way to determine if I would go back to the States for good or continue to live in France. In some ways, I had lost my American roots by living in France for so many years. However, during this period of living part-time in the US and part- time in France I was able to reclaim my American roots, which was very good for me. Financially the best place for me to live was not in the States. I had more security living in France where my husband, children and grandchildren were. In the US, my American family could not assume the responsibility of my presence. Finally, the most important reason was that my husband still lived in France and my duty is to stay near him.

People often asked me why I did not go back and live in the States full-time? Or, which do you prefer, the United States or France? I like both but, I said yes to my husband in 1952 and

I knew I was going to live with him in France. I am still in France where my husband lives, which settles any questions of why, how or when.

In 1982 I was still with the gypsies but I was going back and forth to see my family and living in Grenoble where there was a community called La Saint Croix. That is where my oldest son and daughter-in-law were converted and are drug free. They decided to go to another community. I decided to go to the La Saint Croix community. I stayed in this community for a year and a half and used to go back and forth between the gypsies and my family.

Chapter

7 *A Second Crossroad*

La Saint Croix community was perfect for me, full of young people and people who wanted to live a dedicated, radical Christian life. This community was vibrant like the other new charismatic communities.

After a few years many families in the area did not like what their children were getting involved in, not living like other young people and thought it was too radical. People started to complain to the Bishop and he decided that the community had to stop. It was a shame because it was a very good community, one dedicated to God.

Later, I met a woman named Danielle Bourgeois from a community in Canada, named Solitude Myriam. In January 1987 I went to see this community and learned about people who want to stay faithful in their marriage. I stayed one week with them and I was so happy because it was the first time since 1971 when my husband left me that I found someone to discuss what I was living. She understood because she went through the same thing. Before that, anytime I shared my story with somebody I was frustrated. They could not understand nor accept my way of life, my dedication to God and to my husband.

She suggested that instead of staying in Canada with them, it would be better for me to go back to France, and to another community, while waiting for a similar community, like Solitude Myriam, to start in France. This is a Catholic community, which provides a place where followers who have been divorced yet wanting to stay faithful to their marriage vows - live together. They are philanthropic especially helping others by their example of faith and prayer. Forgiveness, seventy times seven, is key to them as well as growing in faith, hope and love. They evangelize in many countries, parishes and conferences.

As of today, France does not have such a community. In October of 1987, I was accepted into the community of the Beatitudes, in a beautiful area near Orleans. We celebrated all the feast days even the Shabbat. Nobody worked outside the community. So I stayed with that community for two years since one cannot just enter and say I am going to stay forever. You have only one year of apprenticeship. If you want to continue, you have to be a postulant, which takes two years. Finally, after several   years you make your final commitment.

We realized that my first calling was not this community life. My first calling was to my family life. Community came second. My place was not there. Although I thought that my place was with them I realized it was not that. Here I had to choose, in advance, where I wanted to be buried. That was the way it was done in the community of Beatitudes. At that point I decided to buy a plot there, in the centre of France. I will be buried with my husband's family. But, after the first year, again I realized that my place was not in this small community, because here community and evangelization must come before family. It was discerned that my priority was my family and so this community was not for me.

As I have said before, I never make a decision alone it is always with another follower of God and my community helps me find my direction.

My husband's aunt, to whom I was very close, used to live in the centre of France. She had an apartment in the town and before she died I used to visit her often especially while I was in the community near Orleans. So, since my Aunt had passed away and I had visited her often I thought it was time for me to settle down in that area. My Aunt's family agreed that I could stay in her apartment loaning me all her furniture until I found items to replace it.

This was in 1990 when some of the family was still alive. However, like all areas and families, gradually those I knew died or moved to another place. I was alone but, I had adapted to this town, the people knew me and they knew my family. Also, I was involved with the activities in church and town. I was settled there and thought I would stay until my husband called me back or I died. After seven years it became more difficult, eventually I was alone more and more. I really liked this town, I was happy there but as shops and business began to close up it was no longer the place for me to live. I was 72 years old and I realized that it was not good for me to be there, the solitude was too difficult.

I had no family, no more friends, and no more prayer meetings and most importantly no daily mass. I could not handle it anymore and I knew that this was not good for me psychologically. Therefore, I thought it might be time for me to consider a senior citizen's home. However, I knew in my heart that if I was going to one I was not going there to die. Rather, I was going there to live, to continue my life in hope that one day my husband will return to our marriage. No matter where I live

I will continue sharing with people and be useful. I could not live with my children or in the community so I had to find my own place to live, a spiritual place where I would flourish for the rest of my life.

Chapter

8

Wonders of God

I went to Lyon to visit my children and my best friend Danielle. She said, "I cannot understand why you are applying to other homes, in other places in France? Here in Lyon we have the Little Sisters of the Poor." I remember seeing one of these houses in the center of France and I said that it is not for me, I had no desire to live in this type of home. She said, "Just look! Let's go and see."

We went to visit and I was amazed at the feeling I had, all was good. It was a very old house but very nice. What amazed me the most was that the people looked happy. I used to visit a lot of senior citizen homes as a volunteer but I never saw people as happy as they were there. They were so very peaceful. The Mother Superior was happy to see me, as a younger woman who wanted to come to the house they did not hesitate to accept me.

I filled out the application and came back in June. I told the Mother Superior that I would like to come into their home. I wanted to know if there were similar homes in the south of France because the climate of the Lyon region was not good for me. Even though my children live in that area I knew that their lives could change and they may go somewhere else. She gave me a list of seven other houses and advised me to call the one in Nice and see if I could visit.

I contacted the Mother Superior of the Little Sisters of the Poor in Nice and asked to visit for 15 days. I'll always remember that conversation

Mother Superior: "When do you want to come?"

Carmela: "The 15th or 16th of September."

In the morning my son said, "Mom if you are going to stay you must know I can only help you to move on October 15th, or November 22nd. Keep these dates otherwise, I am not here and I cannot help you move to Nice."

I came by train changing in Lyon. It took me two days to arrive in Nice. I took a taxi from the station and was amazed to see the building and the beautiful house. I took a tour of the home and the lovely garden then I saw my room. However, when I went to bed I said this place is not for me. I could not sleep one minute. The train passed behind our property and I was not used to the noise as well as the busy street on the other side of the building. I simply said this place is not for me, I will never adapt and must leave as soon as possible.

That night I slept very little and the next morning I realized that this was the first time I had signed up for something and was actually running away and it was only for fifteen days. I realized I should follow through on my commitment and see how I felt at the end of my visit. That was a Tuesday night; by Wednesday morning I changed my attitude and on Thursday night I asked the Mother Superior, "Do you think I can stay?"

She responded, "Don't you think it is a bit soon to decide?" I said, "I am sure my place is here". It was the intuition in my heart and I was sure it was right.

When I arrived in September they did not have money to transform the building so my room was empty which allowed me to be accepted right away. This is divine Providence. I rushed back to my home to prepare to leave it for good. I did not have much time to dispose of my four-room apartment, sell my car and pack, as well as arrange everything for my funeral (choose my coffin and the color) all of which needed to be done before I entered the senior citizen house.

I did not have much help, but thanks to God, two nuns came once in a while to help me. It was the support I needed. After one week I had a phone call from my son. He asked how I was doing and I said okay but it was very difficult for me. Then he said there was a bit of a change. First, he was not able to come on the 15th of October. Instead, I had to be ready a week earlier. I thought, "My God; this is not possible I will never make it!"

My son said for me not to worry that he would come and help me the day before our departure. He wouldn't have the truck so we would have to use his car. I had no idea how I was going to do that but again my son reassured me not to worry. He suggested I put my bags and boxes in my friend's basement and he would eventually bring them to me. I thought he would never be able to do that. I knew his way of life and felt he would not be able to fulfill such a promise. But, I had no choice. Each time I worried about what was happening to my belongings or, how was I going to manage this move to my new home, this big change in my life I could not sleep.

So, as I have done my entire Christian life, I gave this to the Lord. I just kept filling up the boxes. I found a neighbor who was able to keep most of my things. I sold my car, some furniture and gave away a lot of things, everything I could get rid of. The rest I simply put in boxes to store. I could not take much. When my son arrived to help me we went to a restaurant where my cousin had invited me to lunch. I was still concerned about the approaching deadlines and our long journey as well as the many changes taking place in my life.

By the grace of God on October 8th, the next day at 8:00 AM everything was ready. My son had borrowed a bigger car, which helped immensely and we were off.

It was a long trip from the center of France to Nice. We arrived at 6:00 PM and my son stayed with me overnight. They gave him a room next to mine because the floor was empty. The Mother Superior questioned him, asking if my brain was really working well. She thought I was a little strange. Coming to the home at my age, deciding so fast to stay, she wanted to know if I had all my faculties.

When we were alone, my son advised me to be careful, because these people were not like me, so alive and charismatic. He suggested to me to be low key. The next morning he had to go back to his work. I started moving into my room, unpacking my boxes and settling down. I did not know anybody in Nice and no one knew me. Here, I lost my background and had to find a way to live my new life. I asked one of the helpers if she knew of any prayer groups in Nice. She didn't but thought that a friend of hers may. She was right. I met each Wednesday with this lady and discussed spiritual topics very easily and, she introduced me to many prayer groups.

Senior citizen's home in Nice where I have been living for over 12 years

That's a gift of the Holy Spirit. If you go to a different town and are on your own, ask someone if there is a prayer group, then you will know everyone, like brothers and sisters. I have been introduced to different groups and finally through one found a couple that I had not seen for over 25 years. They were very close to my son and my daughter-in-law. They used to be drug addicts and through God's help were returned to both spiritual and physical health. They were the only people I knew from my previous life. It was wonderful because every Tuesday after work they would pick me up.

They lived in Nice at that time and I would go to there home, have dinner with them and then we would go to our prayer meeting together. I would sleep at their place because at that time I did not have permission to return to the home after 8:00 PM. These small, regular breaks did me a lot of good.

We continued our visits for a number of years and through them I met more people with a shared spiritual quest. Like many good things this wonderful period ended when my friend was transferred to another area for work. We kept in contact but it was not the same. They were like my children and it was nice to find someone who knew me before my new life in Nice. They knew my background, children, my husband and it was like being with family.

Fortunately, I had come to know many people so I still had the opportunity to go out for the evening and attend my prayer groups. This was a change. I was now able to go out anytime and return anytime. Friends would pick me up and like before, we would attend these meetings together and then I would return.

When I arrived my goal was to be a part of the house so I became an "animatrice" (organize activities) with special exercises for older people. However, this was not widely accepted. Some people began to complain, "It is too fast, it hurts too much, and I am too tired". Such negativity was contagious and I realized that I had to have somebody from outside perform such tasks. It was as if jealousy came into play when some residents asked, "Who is she to give us lessons?"

I tried to find real friends in the house but every time I thought somebody would be a friend it just did not work. I remember one girl, who was younger than me, but we clicked right away and she introduced me to people in another church. She became a very good friend and we started attending this church together. One morning she said to me, "You know we cannot be friends you are too different from me". That was it. I couldn't understand because it was a wonderful friendship up until that point. Was I too much for her? I tried every means to find friends, someone just to play cards with and to join me in other activities at night.

Chapter

9

Life in Nice

N ow we have an animatrice with different activities so I do not have to worry about finding friends or keeping busy. However, there is one thing I continue to try to make friends who like fellowship. I hope that one day it will work out. After 7:30 PM everybody rushes back to their room and nobody wants to talk or to play games until it's time to go to sleep. Rather, they prefer to be in their room with the television. Thus, I am in my room with my prayers and my books but without a television and now I have the Internet.

You can feel lonely but thanks to God I can go out at night and I have a telephone. I still pray to find somebody who will become a true friend like the one I had until a few years ago. She came to the house when she was 97 or 98 years old. She was right next-door and was the closest friend I could have ever asked for. She remained so until she died at 102 years old.

She was a gift; a real friend and we were lucky to be able to share everything during our time together.

She was from another generation and a wise woman. I really missed her when she left to return to our Lord and I have never found anyone to take her place. I like everybody and they know me but unfortunately, I have no real friendships here and I think it is hard for some residents to relate to me because I do originate from another culture. I realize that people my age still have that "decalage" or gap.

Carnival in Nice- me as an Indian

When I came to France this country was 25 years behind times as compared to America. This gap still remains in people of my age. That's why I can relate easier to younger people. I realize that explains many things.

Since my husband and I decided in 1961 that we would not expose ourselves to television those who do are living in another dimension; another way of thinking and talking, television is a part of their life. They know about programs and the characters as if it was their families. I am unable to join in such conversations. I understand too that it may be difficult for others to have a relationship with me because I have chosen a life without television etc.

Carnival in Nice- me as a clown

I hoped I would have had better relationships with the Sisters. I thought that they would have more time to speak with me, to visit with me, that we could share our spirituality by praying together. However, with God's help I realized this is not possible because they have their own community life. The 6th and 7th floor is their Convent where they retreat for their fellowship and worship. They are very kind to us, take very good care of us, yet they can't do anymore for us than they already give us, they cannot be our friends the way we may want. That was another illusion that I had to dispel. Sometimes I feel as though I live in solitude here but I know it is a consequence of my choice. I have to accept this solitude because it was my choice, a choice to stay faithful to my calling and my vocation in marriage.

I keep busy because I have a deeper life than I ever had before and I strive to enrich myself as well as my faith. I enjoy listening to music and the radio. People ask me how I keep up with world events. For me it has always been very easy. Since I don't have a television I have to rely on other methods. I have always kept up with the news because people talk about it, and I listen to the news on the radio once a day, I join in such conversations and I read. For the past 2 years, I have had a computer and this allows me to talk to my sisters and family for free. I have time, I am very free and I think I am more helpful praying for the world events than worrying about them. I have some friends who visit me occasionally and I have the opportunity to travel. These visits plus phone calls are always helpful.

And of course, I keep very busy with my prayers. I do not feel useless.

My health is much better here than it has ever been; we have physiotherapists, a pool for physiotherapy, exercise classes and everything to help me to have a better health. This is everything I need right here in Nice. Every two years I go back to the United States, which is an easy voyage from Nice. Also, here I have free bus rides in town so I can walk on the Promenade des Anglais and other places. Due to the rocky shores of Nice I restrict my walking to the wide sidewalks along the Mediterranean and enjoy outings to other beaches with either gravel or sand. We have plenty of activities available and I feel I need to be a part of them even helping others who may be older or less mobile than me. As long as I can go out I am very happy. Unfortunately, many residents are unable to go out and many of their rooms are rather empty. They choose not to bring many of their belongings with them. I am blessed because my room is filled with objects of my faith, mementos of my marriage, family and many other things, which bring me happiness.

A typical day begins with breakfast between 8 AM till 9 AM on our respective floors. French bread, pastries, and coffee are more than sufficient. We then lunch together in the dinning room, which resembles a large restaurant and later we have dinner there. Everybody is not catholic.

The home is for the poor so no one is turned away based on their faith or lack of religion.

Charity Sale

We have two choices of daily mass so my spirit is well served. It is very complete. We have doctors, a dentist and any specialist we may require. My husband gives me approximately 400 Euros a month. Our income goes to the house and we keep 10 percent for pocket money. I keep my bank account that I saved up before I entered. So we have a sense of independence and choice. This allows me to travel and pay for my telephone, computer and periodicals. I was lucky to find such a wonderful place to live and realize that God truly provides for our every need.

I did not get rid of everything because I keep traveling. I need clothes for both hot and cold weather as well as the many events in which I participate. I see my children about twice a year now. Recently, I began volunteering at another senior citizen home. There, I conduct exercise classes once a week, adapted for the elderly and even disabled. Like the other gifts in my life, I appreciate my health and therefore want to share my strengths by helping others.

Since my husband divorced me, we could not adopt our son. Later, when he legally and spiritually, remarried in another church, he and his wife adopted our son so he could have the family name. It was very difficult for me to give up my parental rights yet I knew God would continue to bless my unconditional love and devotion to the Lord as well as my family.

Our son is now living near Lyon and has a teenage daughter. Unfortunately, he has been divorced and he and his first wife have gone on to have many other relationships. I don't judge them rather I live my life as an example of God's purpose of marriage.

Our oldest son was born in New York City and was four months old when we came to France. He is now a mature father of five grown children and has never been divorced. He is a deacon in his Christian community where he and his wife share many responsibilities in the ministry.

As they and their children have grown they no longer need the constant care of a grandmother and have spread their wings, as they should. We remain in regular contact on the phone and I spend Christmases with them.

All is good.

Chapter

10 *Golden Jubilee*

In 2002, I enjoyed a celebration of the jubilee of our marriage. For many years, I have been part of a group, which has a community in Canada, of people who are divorced yet have decided to stay in their marriages. Every year we renew our marriage vows and as a Catholic I do this with a priest or deacon. This aids us to continue to receive the blessings that God has given us and it overflows to other couples and families.

As I approached 50 years of marriage, I wrote to the woman in charge of this community in Canada. I asked her if it would be a good idea to have a celebration since I am the first one in this group to reach this milestone of marriage. She said yes.

In March 2002 I celebrated my Jubilee in Lyon with friends and on April 19th 2002 in Nice. In Nice, I invited people from my prayer groups as well as my many other friends. I sent invitations but did not ask for a response. I had no idea who would attend and who would not be able to join me.

The ceremony was at 3:30 pm on Saturday afternoon in a beautiful church, a monastery, in Cimiez, Nice. The Priest of the parish asked me how many people I thought would attend. When I said that I had no idea he said we can do it one of two ways. If there are more than 30 people we will go to the monastery "Our Lady of the Angels". If there are less than 30 people we will go to another, smaller chapel.

Jubilee 2002 monastery in Nice

Young women in Lyon who live a similar calling

A week before the celebration I began to receive many phone calls. People were apologizing that they could not come, some even sending flowers. Yet at the church there were over 60 people. I was so amazed. I wish I had it all on videotape. I felt I lived a biblical story. Jesus said if you leave your home, your friends, etc. you would find that you have a hundred more. I left everything and I found 60 people who love and support me. Everything we needed was there and the ceremony was wonderful. I had so many gifts it was like a wedding. I even have a short part of the celebration on video and the entire event on an audiotape.

Jubilee in Lyon

Since I married my husband and I believe with all my heart that God does not approve nor accept divorce, I never make an important decision or move without my husband's knowledge of it. Therefore, he knew about this ceremony. I do that for a very special reason because our husbands are a protection for us. God made husbands to protect their wives. A wife who is not protected is vulnerable.

Despite my husband leaving me, I decided to remain a loving and submissive wife, not as a slave but consciously submitting, if there is a situation where we can not agree. Women are one of God's most amazing creations and they flourish with the love and support of their husbands. Without her husband to protect her she may hurt herself trying to handle everything, perhaps even trying to control everything, have her own way, or always trying to be right. Working together as a unit is God's will for marriage.

Because of my choice and my faith to remain in my marriage, God's gift to me is my husband, I sleep very well at night. I have a clear conscience and rejoice in the joy of living each day as God intends me to.

THE STORY OF TWO JUBILEES
OF OUR MARRIAGE

March 2nd 2002
Lyon, France
&
April 20th at
Nice, France
(Francisan Monastery of Cimiez)

A JUBILEE, an occasion to Jubilate!
Jubilate, that is to say,
welcome the joy of God,
to live by that joy
and hand it down to all who surround
us or with whom we are in
touch one way or another.
May my renewing of my marriage
vows be for God's Glory and to give
praise and thanks to the Lord
for His faithfulness and grace during the
ups and downs of these past 50 years!

During these celebrations I spoke of my marriage history, renewed my marriage vows and received the blessing of a Priest at Lyon and of a Deacon at Nice.

This is what I said during the ceremony:

When I arrived at Nice, about 5 years ago, I knew no one and yet I feel that I have been living the accomplishment of God's promise according to Christ's words: "To you who leave home, brothers, sisters, country for my sake and for the Gospel, I will grant you the hundredfold."

Thank you all for being here. For those who do not know what I live in my state of marriage, I will explain in a few words. You know that I am American; I married a French man in 1952 and arrived in France in 1953. On our wedding day I said "Yes" to my husband, in God's promise to the both of us at that time and all along these 50 years!

After 20 years of marriage my husband began saying "No", but God's "Yes" continues! My "Yes" continues and I live in expectation of these words with which the Lord has encouraged me for the past 30 years: "Continue to hope against all hope"

"Man cannot separate what God has joined together"

"Have I not told you that if you believe you will see the glory of God?"

"Forgive 70 times 7"

"The Lord will not be late in accomplishing all his promises"

"Listen to me, people with hardened hearts, enemies of righteousness!"

"My justice is approaching, it is near; and my salvation is not far off"

My salvation will be for Zion, And my Glory in Israel.   Many people ask me this question: "When will your husband return? I answer: "Soon"! Like the return of the Lord, we know not the day nor the hour, I wait with joyful hope!

Another thing I want to explain is why I renew my marriage vows. After about 10 years after my husband left me, I discovered a community: 'SOLITUDE MYRIAM', comprised of people having suffered from divorce and desire to remain faithful to their marriage vows. In this community, like Priests and Sisters, we renew our "Yes" in church in the presence of a Priest or Deacon.

And every year, I make my renewal in the presence of a Priest or Deacon, wherever I am. This year being the 50th anniversary, I want it to be more joyful. Another reason why I am happy to live this moment with you is because all the Sacraments with all their "Yeses" overflow on the whole Church and on couples who are surrounding me today and their families.

My prayer and my happiness would be that all the couples you know may be blessed by this celebration, for the Glory of the Lord.

I am now going to renew my vows. Oh! There is one more important thing that I would like to add because I feel it is a gift of God for everyone! When "YES" is pronounced at Marriage, God fills our hearts with his Love. His love therefore is always in my husband's heart for me as it is in mine for him; this is why I feel blessed and joyful, because I know that, in spite of appearances (his absence), I know that my husband loves me! I believe it and I rejoice in the thought of it! I continue to love him and I am ready to welcome him back!

Renewal of my marriage vows: In the presence of the Blessed Trinity, of Mary Mother of the Church, of our brother and sisters present here and all those present in our hearts I, Carmela Maria, united with my husband, I renew my vows to live faithful to Christ, faithful to the church, I promise to live the virtues of charity and joy and fidelity according to the spirit of Myriam Victoire. I count on your grace O Lord to live my promise deeply and I ask you to pour out your blessing on my husband, my children, grandchildren and on the whole church and the whole world.

Jubilee in Nice

PRAYER OF BLESSING

(Ritual prayer for fiancee,
adapted for renewal
of marriage vows)
(unofficial translation)

O God, who by your sovereign power has made all things from nothing; who has commanded the first elements of the universe, after having created man to your image, you formed the woman to be his inseparable help and companion; you who brought the body of the woman from the very flesh of man, to teach us that it is never lawful to separate that which, by your will has the same origin; O God who has made the union of spouses by such an elevated mystery, that marriage is the figure of the union of Jesus Christ with his church; O God by who a woman is united to man and who grants such a great benediction to this union, which has never been abolished, neither by original sin nor the punishment of deluge (The flood at Noah's time): look kindly upon your servant who, at the moment of this consecration, asks for the help of your protection. May the yoke she is preparing to accept be a yoke of love and peace; faithfulness and chaste, may she be renewed in Jesus Christ and follow forever the example of holy women. May she be amiable with her husband as Rachel, as wise as Rebecca; may she have long life and be as faithful as Sarah within herself and all her actions. May Satan, author of prevarication find nothing in her that belongs to him; may she always remain firm in faith and in the observance of your commandment; uniquely united to her husband, may she flee any illicit commerce; may her weakness rest on the strength of discipline; may she be modest, filled with heavenly desires; grant her a happy fecundity, may her life be pure and innocent, may she come safely to the kingdom of heaven with all the saints. May both spouses live to see the children of their children to the third and fourth generations and may they grow together happily to old age.

Through Jesus Christ our Lord. Amen.

BENEDICTION
OF HER WEDDING BANDS

Increase O Lord your love for her and her husband and make them holy. They gave each other these wedding bands as a sign of fidelity may they grow more and more by the grace of the sacrament by Jesus Christ our Lord and Savior Amen.

11 *Current Relationships*

L etters to my husband his answer:

My Dear Husband,

Tonight April 4, 2006 in our prayer group, we are having an evening of reconciliation where those who felt like writing a letter to God or to a friend or to their children or to their husband or wife etc. to ask them to forgive me. I don't remember asking you explicitly to forgive me for not being able to live up to your expectations during the many years we lived together and even after our separation so tonight "I ask you to forgive me."

God Bless you

Love,
Carmela Maria

Tuesday, 8 April 2006

Dear Carmela,

Your letter arrived just as we were coming back from a retreat in an Orthodox Monastery where the Abbey is my second wife's godfather. I neither don't remember "asking you explicitly for forgiving me for not having been able to live up to your expectations during the many years we lived together and even after our separation." I know I have been the cause for you of long and cruel sufferings. So I ask you to forgive me. I wish you a good and happy trip to the United States.

God Bless You.

Him.

Letter to his second wife and her answer

My Dear Friend,

As I have written to my husband this evening in our prayer group, we are having an "Evening of Reconciliation" where those who felt like writing a letter to God or to a friend or to their children or to their husband or wife etc. to ask them to forgive me.

I don't remember if I have already done so, so tonight- "I ask you to forgive me because I have not been able to live up to your expectations- I kiss you and ask God to bless you.

Carmela Maria

My Dear Carmela Maria,

Your letters have deeply touched us. Me too I have to ask you to forgive me for all the suffering that you have had... We thought a lot about all this suffering but we could not do otherwise-. We could only follow the call of our destiny. May God bless you and fill you each day with his peace.

Your Friend

---

27 April 2006

Letter from Carmela Maria to both of them

(I received your letters very late because the postmen were on strike)

I received your asking me to forgive you with deep emotion and joy and to complete this new step, I say to you "my husband in the name of Jesus Christ I forgive you" and " in the name of Jesus Christ my friend I forgive you" and this is the way we conquer all evil by good. For the Glory of God and our salvation. I kiss both of you and I ask God to bless us all and to forgive us.

Love

Carmela Maria

Romans 12:21

> Verse 21 "Do not be overcome by evil, but overcome evil with good."
> Matthew 5-23-24
> Verse 23 "Therefore, if you are offering your gift at the altar and there remember that your brother has something against you, 24 leave your gift there in front of the altar. First go

and be reconciled to your brother; then come and offer your gift."

12 *Fidelity Documents*

T he key to love is forgiveness.

THIS INTERVIEW WAS DONE
BY PHONE BETWEEN
CARMELA MARIA
AND A JOURNALIST FROM
THE COMMUNITY OF THE BEAUTITUDES:

Carmela Maria is living right now in the center of France. Her married children live in Lyon, and are in service to the Lord. Carmela, American by birth, has been divorced from her French husband for more than 20 years. Her husband who had lost the faith of his birth was diverted by another woman toward "new age" spirituality and other paths. Carmela has spent two years in the "Community of the Beatitudes".

Michael: You have been separated from your husband for a number of years and you have gone through a variety of trials and tribulations and stages along the way. How did this long journey begin?

Carmela: This started in August 1971, when another woman came into the life of my husband. My husband used to live 15 days with her, and 15 days with me. This went on for two years. Finally I decided to step aside. My husband had no peace and he was living in a hell of increasing pain. But I held words of hope in my heart, which I have never forgotten: "Man cannot separate what God has united" and "What is impossible for me is possible for God". And I have continued to forgive- to forgive 70 times 7. No one knew about our situation, because to do so would complicate the situation even further.

Michael: In the face of all this suffering, where do you see the hope in what you are actually living?

Carmela: Yes, there was plenty of suffering for all four of us: my husband and I, as well as the other woman whose husband divorced her. Yes I have been through many painful stages and I live in the happy expectation of being united again with him and with the Lord. I was recently filled with a new out pouring of love for my husband, which fills me with hope, joy and peace. Often, divorced people strive to forget their suffering and their spouse. Consequently, they deprive themselves of the special grace of their marriage. Solitude I fear no more, by living in faith and hope. I still love my husband. His photos are everywhere in the house. I will not forget him and do love him in spite of everything.

Michael: Do you feel that your faith is separating you from your husband, or is it rather helping you in the hope of restoration of your marriage through God?

Carmela: My faith in marriage really bothered him. At first he respected me for my faith in marriage and understood this on a spiritual level. But gradually he and the other woman were no longer able to live this way other than on a human level. Two years ago I suggested we spend Christmas with the grandchildren. I was ready to see him. He told me that he was not ready to accept this situation, where I continue to say I am his wife in the eyes of God. He would like to be friends, but he could not understand my fidelity to him, and why I was so stubborn in insisting that I was his wife.

Michael: It is difficult to forgive when the situation continues for such a long time. Have you continued to progress or, are there times when you slip backwards?

Carmela: Forgiving is a battle. I have faced many injustices, but it is through prayer, that I am able to forgive. I want to forgive and God gives me the strength and grace to do it. Like Mary, who was able to have a child without knowing a man, because the Lord made it possible, God gives me grace minute by minute, so that I can forgive, with the hope that it might reach my husband. When I go to confession, I think of the sins of both my husband and I and I offer them to God. He is ready to have compassion on us and reunite us. To have compassion for a partner is a must.

Michael: **As a Friend of the Lamb in the community what is your mission and your state as a divorced person?**

Carmela: I will not say that I am a divorcee, but that it is my husband who divorced me. I have never asked for any legal action against my husband, I have remained ever faithful to my husband in every way. I do love him and I have a great deal of respect for him. I keep him aware of everything important that is happening in my life. And I will remain faithful to him; come what may. Yet I have a mission, which is to offer my suffering for all the couples, who face hardship. It is the communion of Saints that keeps my children, my husband and I united. When I see couples coming to Bethany on retreats I admire their happy faces, and I feel so happy myself.

I sent a copy of this document to Pope Jean Paul II and this was his answer 15 days later with a gift that was a medallion of the Virgin Mary and the Pope.

The Vatican, 23 November 1994
Secretary of State
First Section
General Affairs

The Secretary of State has a pleasure to inform you that the Holy Father was touched by your itinerary and testimony of fidelity in marriage. He assures you that he will pray for you and your intentions and for all those people who are dear to you.

With all his heart, the Pope bestows on you and yours the blessings of the Lord.

Mgr. L. Sandri

Assesseur

Letter to present Pope and his response
10 January 2006
Dear Holy Father,

In 1994, I wrote a short personal letter to our Holy Father Jean-Paul II, to thank him for his Encyclical letter: 'The Splendor of the Truth' which confirmed and strengthened me to continue living our marriage in fidelity-and as I did for him, I am sending you a short testimony of God's fidelity in our marriage since 1952 (54 years of marriage).

Most of all I am writing to you to inform you of what many men and women of the world are now living.

Enclosed is my testimony and information for "Ministries for Marriage Restoration"!

I am very happy that God answered my prayers for electing you as Pope for His church today and I pray for all your intentions.

I wish you a good and Holy New Year 2006 for the glory and our salvation. Alleluiah!

Carmela Maria

THE VATICAN
24 January 2006

The Secretary of State is pleased to inform
you that the Holy Father received your letter
dated January 10th and was very impressed
by your decision to continue to live your actual
situation with fidelity to the Gospel and the
Church teachings, in the sight of God.

The Pope, formulates in his prayer all best
wished for you and invites you to continue
on courageously to follow Christ, to whom he
asks for you his courage and his peace.

Confiding you to the intercession of the
Blessed Virgin Mary, Our Lady of the Alliance,
the Holy Father invokes on you and all your
loved ones, an abundnce of divine Blessings.

Mgr Gabriel Caccia Assessor

Rejoice Marriage Ministry
PO Box 11242
Pompano Beach, FL
http://www.rejoiceministries.org

Dear Pastor,

With the trauma of divorce attacking fifty percent of all marriages, even within the church, it must happen to you often. A hurting spouse makes an appointment and comes to your study for marriage counseling. What do you do? Do you listen to the circumstances, and then suggest an attorney, and pass along information on a divorce recovery class, or do you share the hope for hurting marriages that can be found in the scriptures?

We have been asked to provide you with information on the role the Pastor can have in marriage restoration, God's alternative to divorce. On the enclosed recording we share our testimony and beliefs, as well as the hope that God can provide for every marriage. You are welcome to make copies, as the Lord leads.

In the early 1980's my wife, Charlyne, found herself sitting in many pastor's studies, sharing her story of nineteen years of marriage and three children. She shed tears as she told her story of a husband's unfaithfulness and abuse. Instead of asking the Lord how He saw me, she was taking surveys of every pastor and counselor who would listen. The answers she heard were all the same; "Get a divorce."

It took our family going through a divorce, and all the associated damage to our precious children, before the Lord touched this prodigal, in response to the faithful prayers of a wife, standing with Him and praying for marriage restoration. Two years after our divorce, we were remarried in our Pastor's office.

Many studies have demonstrated the disadvantages that follows children of divorced parents for their entire lives. They may make poorer grades, have less chance at graduating from college, make less money, have a better chance of being arrested, and have increased difficulty keeping their own marriage together.

Divorce is said to be America's biggest

socio-economic problem. Much is now being said about divorce, but what is the solution? It is not to make divorce more amicable through divorce recovery classes, where both spouses go on to eventually find new spouses, in marriages that have an even higher chance of failure. It is not in teaching our hurting children how to cope.

God designed the family to be man and woman, loving each other, and raising children together, so that each member of the family serves God. Is that even possible any longer? Yes it is! The men and women you counsel need to hear there is a better option than divorce, and the accompanying lifelong problems. They need to find an altar, not an attorney, and to enter into a personal relationship with the Lord, allowing Him to first change them.

This process is not instant, but neither were the problems. The true answers are found not in court, but in the Bible. God has made His people thousands of promises, and He has kept everyone of them.

May wounded spouses who turn to you

hear there is an alternative to divorce. Please do not hesitate to contact us if we can help minister to your families in any way. May the Lord continue to bless your ministry for Him. In His great love,

Bob and Charlyne Steinkamp
Rejoice in the Lord always.
I will say it again: Rejoice!
Philippians 4:4

A Stander's Affirmation
(Standers are those who stand in fidelity to
their marriage in this way.
These prayers can be said once a week by all
the Standers around the world.)

I am standing for the healing of my marriage!
I will not give up, give in, give out or give over,
until that healing takes place. I made a vow,
I said the words, I took a ring, I gave myself,
I trusted God, and said the words...
and meant the words...
in sickness and in health, in sorrow
and in joy, for better or for worse,
for richer or for poorer,
in good times and in bad.
So, I am standing now, and will not sit down,

let down, slow down, calm down, fall down,
or be down until the breakdown is torn down!
I refuse to put eyes on outward circumstances,
or listen to prophets of doom,
or buy into what is trendy, worldly,
popular, convenient, easy, quick,
thrifty or advantageous...
nor will I settle for a cheap imitation
of God's real thing, nor will I seek to lower
God's standard, twist God's will, rewrite God's
Word, violate God's covenant, or accept what
God hates, namely divorce!
In a world of filth, I will stay pure;
surround by lies I will speak the truth;
where hopelessness abounds
I will hope in the God;
where revenge is easier I will bless instead of
curse; and where the odds are stacked against
me, I will trust in God's faithfulness.
I am a stander, and I will not compromise,
quarrel or quit. I have made the choice,
set my face, entered the race,
believed the Word,
and trusted God for all the outcome.
I will allow neither the reaction of my
spouse, nor the urging of my friends,
nor the advice of my loved ones, nor
economic hardship, nor the prompting of the

devil to make me let up, slow up, or give up
until my marriage is healed!

Malachi Chapter 2:13-16

[13]"This is another thing you do: you drown
the LORD's altar with tears, weeping and
wailing, because He no longer accepts the
offerings you bring him..

[14]"You ask why he no longer accepts them?
It is because he knows that you have broken
your promise to the wife you married when
you were young. She was your partner, and
you have broken your promise to her although
you promised before God that you would be
faithful to her.

[15]"Didn't God make you one body and
spirit with her? What was his purpose in this?
It was that you should have children who are
truly God's people. So make sure that none of
you breaks his promise to his wife.

[16]"I hate divorce," says the LORD God of
Israel, "I hate it when one of you does such a
cruel thing to his wife. Make sure that you do
not break your promise to be faithful to your
wife.

From the desk of Dr. Bob Moorehead

Spiritual Warfare For _____

Shattering Your Strongholds From

"In the name of Jesus Christ, I bind _____'s body, soul and spirit to the will and purposes of God for his life. I bind _____'s mind, will and emotions to the will of God. I bind him to the truth and to the blood of Jesus. I bind him to the mind of Christ, that the very thoughts, feelings and purposes of His heart would be within his thoughts.

"I bind _____'s feet to the path of righteousness that his steps would be steady and sure. I bind him to the work of the cross with all of its mercy, grace, love, forgiveness and dying to self.

"I loose every old wrong, ungodly pattern of thinking, attitude, desire, belief, motivation, habit and behavior from him. I tear down, crush, smash and destroy every stronghold associated with these things. I loose the strongholds of unforgiveness, fear, and distrust from him.

"I loose the power and effects of deceptions and lies from him. I loose the confusion and blindness of the god of this world from _____'s mind that has kept him from seeing the light of the gospel of Jesus Christ. I call forth every precious word of scripture that has ever entered his mind and heart that it would rise up in power in him.

"In the name of Jesus, I loose the power and effects of any harsh or hard words (word curses) spoken to, about or by _____'s. I loose all generational bondages and associated strongholds from _____'s I loose all effects and bondages from him that may have been caused by mistakes I have made. Father in the name of Jesus, I crush, smash and destroy generational bondages of any kind from mistakes made at any point between generations. I destroy them right here, right now. They will not bind and curse any more members of this family.

"I bind the strong man Satan, that I may spoil his house, taking back every material and spiritual possession he has wrongfully taken from _____. I loose the enemy's influence over every part of his body, soul and spirit. I loose, crush smash and destroy every evil device he may try to bring into sphere of influence during this day. I bind and loose these things in Jesus' name. He has given me the keys and the authority to do so. Thank you Lord, for the truth. Amen"

"GOD HAS RELEASED ME"
BY Tim Coody

Have you ever considered the statement, "God has released me to ...? Usually it comes in the form of "God has released me to remarry." I find this kind of thinking to be nothing short of amazing. With a flick of the tongue, the changeless word of God has been abrogated by something as fickle and cloudy as human thought and intuition.

What's even more amazing is that we stand for it in the Church. "Well, if God released them to remarry, even if the Bible says they are not eligible, who am I to disagree with God?" but my question for these people is this: "Who are you to boldly embrace what God has clearly forbidden?"

Consider this clear command for Jesus, "Anyone who divorces his wife and marries another woman commits adultery, and the man who marries a divorced woman commits adultery." (Luke 16:18) Jesus clearly defines the behaviours that constitute the sin of adultery, but many in the churches today don't live His definition.

The definition of adultery that Jesus gives us in the Bible is built on the concept of covenant. The Jezebel spirit that dominates our society today also gives us a definition for adultery, but hers is built on the sandy soil of a civil judge's authority, not on the bedrock of God's word. For some reason, many in the churches today have accepted Jezebel's definition of adultery and rejected Jesus' definition. For the most part, the American Church is using her dictionary to define terms, not His. Isn't that bizarre?

We seem to be able to define other sins accurately, but we can't seem to get it right on adultery. Can you imagine a cowboy from the old west saying "Slim, I've been admiring your horse for a long time now, hoping that God would give it to me, and I wanted to inform you that God has now released me to take you horse. Slim might say "That's interesting, Bill, because God just released me to shoot you if you get on my horse, and if you survive, the town is going to help me hang you because you would be a horse thief." When someone steals our horse we call a spade a spade, but if they steal our wife we get confused and go dumb.

God has clearly communicated to us in Luke 16:18, and many other verses, that remarriage while our first spouse remains alive constitutes the sin of adultery but people don't say, "God has released me to commit adultery with him or her," because it would sound foolish. So they say, "God has released me to remarry," because no one ever calls them out on it anymore.

Many Americans churches simply refuse to define adultery the way Jesus does; therefore, well-meaning but deluded Christians, tell us that God has released them to commit adultery. Their mouth says that Jesus is Lord, but their behaviour says that Jezebel is. Why do we so easily tolerate this insanity in the Church? What's happening to us?

Hopefully, the Lord will return for us before we get to the point that we hear people in the church say "God released me to kill my boss or steal from my neighbor." One sin seems to have magically avoided condemnation in the Church today: adultery.

No one in their right mind would give you a pass if you said, "God has freed me to steal my neighbor's horse." But if you said, "God has freed me to steal my neighbour's wife, we don't even blink. We've been bullied by Jezebel into silence.

What is it about the sin of adultery that makes us all get stuck and stupid? It reminds me of AIDS in the 80's. It became the only disease in the world with "civil rights." Only the Lord knows how many people died because of confidentiality of the infected individual superseded the safety of a potential victim to be informed of the danger. No other disease has ever been allowed such immunity, but for reasons that I won't get into here, a diseases was placed in a protected class. What happens to people who begin to protect diseases' exposure? They get sick and die. The same thing happens to Christians who protect certain sins from exposure.

Adultery is the only sin I know of that enjoys a protected status within the Church. We found that we couldn't expose it or discuss it, much less confront it. How did this happen to us? Why did we get so blind when it comes to adultery in the Church? It's a spiritual issue. The spirit of Jezebel threatens if we dare speak is on this issue... "You'll lose your family, friends, church, income etc." She's hoping we'll stay quiet in cowardly silence while she pilfers the treasures of our marriages and families.

But Christian, I urge you to fight for your "lunch money" the next time this spiritual bully comes after it. If we continue to cave in regarding adultery, who knows what dishonor she'll demand from us next. Will she demand that we perform abortions in the sanctuary? It's time for the Church to stand and be counted or risk becoming totally irrelevant. Jesus told us what happens to salt when it looses its saltiness. It is "thrown out and trampled by men."

A prayer to the Holy Spirit
Veni Creator
Come, Creator Spirit

Visit the souls of the faithful
And fill with heavenly grace
The hearts which you have created
You are called the comforter
Gift of the most high God
Source of living water, fire, love
And spiritual unction of the souls
Oh you the spirit of seven gifts
The finger of God's right hand
You are the promise of The Father
Enriching our tongue with speech
Enlighten our minds with your light
Inflame our hearts with your love
Strengthen the weakness of our flesh
By your abiding power.
Drive far from us the wicked enemy
And grant us serene peace:
Thus guided and led by you
We shall avoid all evil.
Through you may come to know
The Father and the Son
And grant that we may ever believe in you
The Spirit of them both.
Glory be to God the Father

And to the Son arisen from the dead
And the Holy Paraclete.
Forever and ever. Amen

Send forth your Spirit and they shall be created.
And you shall renew the face of the earth. Oh God who did instruct the hearts of the faithful.
By the light of the Holy Spirit, grant that, by that same spirit we may know what is right and ever rejoice in his consolation.
Through Christ our Lord. Amen.
Let go and Let God control everything

This was taken from a Biblical calendar, author unknown.
Philippians 4: 6-7
6"Do not be anxious about anything, but in everything, by prayer and petition, with thanksgiving, present your requests to God.
7And the peace of God, which transcends all understanding, will guard your hearts and your minds in Christ Jesus."

He said have no worry for anything. There is no room then for any worry even what we think is legitimate. This does not tell us or give us any reason to be indifferent or careless, it does not allow us to let everything go as it wants: but Paul adds, but in all things expose your request to God in prayers and supplication and with thanksgiving.

This is a way that is traced out for the believer in his difficulties.

He does not look to debate with his problem, he does not look for help from the world to overcome but he goes to God, he prays ~ he pleads with God and thanks Him.

How can we already thank God before receiving the answers to our prayer? Yes we can even if the difficulty is still there it is no longer in our hands but in God's hands.

Then God's peace that nothing can trouble will keep the hearts, minds and thoughts of those who wait on God.

We have cast all our burdens at the foot of God's throne where all the troubles of the entire world can neither shake nor move.

These exhortations are not written for special occasions or to help those who are saturated or crushed with problems and worries and trials.

It is for each one of us and for everyday. Keep this safely hidden in our hearts and taste the joy of the Lord and His peace no matter what is happening. Let us wait in joyful hope for the return of our Lord and Savior Jesus Christ.

Chapter

13 *Spiritual Legacy*

This testament helps me continuously to be focused on the truth - the essential! Come Holy Spirit, Creator blest, and in our hearts take up thy rest;

Come with thy grace and heavenly aid
To fill the hearts which thou hast made
O comfort blest, to thee we cry,
Thou heavenly gift of God most High;
Thou font of life, Fire of love,
And sweet anointing for above.
Praise be to thee, Father and Son,
And Holy Spirit, Three in One;
And may the Son on us bestow
The gifts that from the spirit flow.
Spirit of the living God
Fall afresh on us
Melt us ~ Mold us
Fill us ~ Use us
Spirit of the living God fall afresh on us
So we can serve the Lord our God.
Let go and let God control everything.
And believe that he is doing so right now.

In 1979, when visiting the United States, it was the first time I heard people saying, "Things are so bad they can not get any worse!" This is my personal testimony of what I have seen and experienced in a dialogue between God and me in prayer since 1982

In 1982 ~ USA visit, I received this insight. The situation here is humanly impossible to cope with (and now even worse here and everywhere else).

My God, My God have mercy on us ~ forgive us. We are reaping what we have sowed and it's getting more and more horrible ~ confused ~ distorted ~ polluted ~ painful ~ unjust. We have all lost or are losing our identity of "Sons of God" ~ losing our identity of man ~ woman ~ children ~ unisex ~ wife ~ mother ~ father ~ husband ~ grandparent ~ confusion of roles brother ~ sister.

Profane everything that is sacred.
We're drowning in this confusion of doubt, of disorder, of unbelief ~ ungratefulness ~ fear ~ agitation ~ sickness ~ tribulation ~ dangers ~ burn-out ~ fears of all kinds ~ false prophets and anti-Christ ~ anti Catholic Church ~ anti-

marriage and anti-sacrament. Unless we are ready and willing to admit that we're wrong ~ that we are stuck and lost and that we are going in a wrong direction ~ and are willing to help each other become what God meant us to be instead of accusing each other ~ justifying each other ~ judging each other ~ complaining about each other (but keep forgiving and forgetting in Christ and by Christ) unless we stop: analyzing each other and giving human advice and stop admiring each other instead of seeing what God can do with anyone who desires to be changed and used by him for His glory! His way!

~ Not by trying to save each other in another way than JESUS AS LORD AND SAVIOUR (I'm stuck Jesus please help me, we're stuck Jesus please help us right now.)

~ It's hopeless everywhere!

~ We have gone too far from God and His plan. (It's my fault or I deserve or I need what's happening to me.) (God's tough love)

But Dear God because of your Greatness because of your name and your promises:

~ God have mercy on us- O God help us. Thank you.

~ Get us out or get us through each minute.

Thank you.

~ Show us what to do and think and say now. Thank you.

~ Show us what not to do and think or say right now. Thank you.

Father forgive us, we don't realize what we have done and are still doing. We are so blind and full of illusions about you and about ourselves.

Jesus, I mourn and weep with you, my heart is full of sadness and anguish. If they only knew and I never forget how good ~ how wonderful ~ how perfect is your love and your plan for us, but we and they have been brainwashed into something else ~ programmed ~ polluted ~ confused Christians ~ trapped Christians. We are more like "puffed up specks of dusts" who want to take your place! We have become "Pagan" Christians. My God ~ My God ~ Get us out of the "hell" we have made of our lives ~ our world- our families ~ our churches ~ our couples and our children.

Thank you.

Father make us and keep us one in you
Thank you Father – you're getting us out and
through right this minute so that the world
will know you have sent us your Son Jesus. I
believe and I know and I proclaim and confess
that:

Jesus is the only way

Jesus is the only truth.

Jesus is the only life in abundance.

Come Lord Jesus Come! Come Holy Spirit
Come into the hearts and lives of all of us
twisted ~ messed up ~ burned out ~ polluted
~ confused ~ trapped and "Pagan" Christians,
catering more and more to our fleshly nature.
I have to give you continually this burden
which is too much for us – for me to handle.

On the cross, I believe, you nailed this sin
of the world (this insecurity, this suffering,
this garbage ~ confusion ~ fear ~ agitation ~
disorder) and conquered it and set us and me
free to live again in spite of everything and
everyone who have rejected what you have
said and done.

Praise the Lord! Our God Reigns! He's in
charge and He knows what He is doing.

JESUS IS LORD! Shabbat Shalom. "All is accomplished" every knee shall bow and every tongue confess that JESUS CHRIST IS LORD!

And Mary is our Queen and Mother-Alleluia

In August 1986 ~ Received this insight from God and since then it has been confirmed more and more and everywhere.

Don't give up or give in to anything else but Jesus. Let go and let God take over minute by minute. Only Jesus, who is alive standing by my side, your side, our side, his side, her side, their side can cope with this amount of "garbage", of pollution of mind, body and soul ~ of suffering ~ of insecurity ~ of fear of confusion ~ of agony ~ of agitation, anxiety, "rat race", "dead bodies", "gray sickness" - false prophets and anti-Christ ~ Jesus and only Jesus who is alive can cope with this garbage and even more ~ because on the Cross He also conquered this sin, suffering, sickness, evil, death, garbage and disorder of yesterday, today and tomorrow. Everything is accomplished!

This is the Lamb of God who takes away the sins of the world ~ yesterday, today and tomorrow! Rejoice!

At every mass ~ day after day after day after day in the whole world ~ that's what is really going on until He comes back in "All His Glory" ~ with a New Heaven and a New Earth and gives us all a New Body ~ like His Resurrected Body ~ like the Blessed Mother's Body which was assumed to Heaven ~ Come Lord Jesus Come! "Yes I am coming soon!!"

Lord, I refuse to leave this church ~ mass ~ prayer time etc. the same way I came in. Thank you Father, Son and Holy Spirit.

Alleluia!

The weaker we become humanly speaking ~ the stronger we become if we just trust and lean and cling on the Lord more and more ~
I trust you Jesus
I love you Jesus
I need you Jesus

They all need you. We all need you Jesus.

I thank you Jesus.
I praise you Jesus

But we have to spend time with Him and His Word more and more so He can heal us ~ love us ~ forgive us ~ deliver us ~ restore us ~ protect us and fill us with all the power of His Holy Spirit more and more and more to live ~ one day at a time ~ one minute at a time ~ one second at a time! Then believe that we have received what we have asked for ~ positive faith destroys negative faith!

Our God reigns! He knows all the Why's? How's? When's and Where's? Of our lives ~ He wants the best for us! After all we were created for His pleasure! And not for this world and the way that we have twisted everything and everyone. No wonder we feel and are frustrated in one way or another everywhere ~ "all defeated."

Jesus is really in charge and one day every knee shall bow and every tongue will confess that JESUS CHRIST is Lord. You don't have to give up! Don't give in! Because the strife is over ~ the battle is won ~ live in the Victory in Jesus the Son! He is alive ~ He is coming again! Alleluia!!

Come Lord Jesus Come. Please place your loving and powerful hands right now on each and every one of us and deliver us from all this agony ~ all this vain way of living and thinking and action of this world ~ that we have handed down to them and to each other from generation to generation. Please forgive. Please help us dear JESUS! Come Holy Spirit ~ Come ~ "Yes I am coming soon!" Alleluia!

Thank you God ~ Praise God from Whom All blessings Come and Come and Come!- "Keep doing good. For whatever and whenever and wherever he gives me the grace and strength to do so."

~ "In the Kingdom of God all this is like nothing."

~ "Jesus has already conquered all this!"

~ "In the name of Jesus I let go and let God take care of me and them and everyone and everything and I turn the page. In the name of JESUS I cast out Satan and all his lies."

~ "Come Lord Jesus wipe out all this evil in me and in everyone that you have already conquered on the Cross. Thank you I believe it is done! Alleluia!

This is the Lamb of God who "takes away" this sin, sickness, suffering, garbage abnormal relationships, lack of positive faith, hope, love and agony of this world. Place all this "prayer after prayer" "mass after mass" under your feet as a "ladder"

Maranatha!!!

Matthew: 24 verse 22: ~ "Because of the intercessors and the elect I will shorten these days."
~ "Lord, we're all in such a "humanly hopelessly situation" and you tell me "Great!" "That's wonderful!" "Everything is just fine!" "Now I can do something ~ I can and am coming to help all those who belong to me and admit and know that they need me and are suffering because of me!!

(See Psalm 12:5)
Just keep on Praising me and Trusting me and saying "Great!" "That's wonderful!" JESUS has already won the Victory!!! and He is coming back soon in All His Glory and Power and Love and Truth and Victory!!

Our God Reigns! He has a perfect control of everyone and everything!!

HE IS LORD!!

I am returning now in what seems to be the same situation but I am not like I was yesterday nor even the past minute. Thank you Jesus – You are alive!! It is no longer I who can live, suffer, act, pray, or die etc. etc. but Christ in me and I in Him!!

Praise to You Holy God – Three in One!

Thank you for giving me your Mother to be a wonderful Mother to me and for all of us!

Thank you for your cousin John the Baptist and St. Thomas Moore, who knew God's perfect plan for marriage and had the courage not to compromise God's perfect plan for humanity to live God's way.

Now my Dear Carmela, my gentle faithful one ~ you're God's delight. Don't worry about how you and others are going to cope with everything and everyone in this twisted-humanly impossible situation" ~ everywhere!

You will never make it ~ They will never make it!"

Only JESUS who is alive and lives in you can do it His Way ~ Alleluia ~ and I live in Him, by Him and for Him for the Glory of God and Our Salvation.

My God, My God, why have we forsaken you and your ways to Peace ~ Joy ~ Happiness and Victory ~ in Love and Truth and Justice. Have mercy on us because of your Name, Your Greatness, Your Love and Your Glory.

"Father into your hands I commend my spirit, my household, all your church and everything that is happening right now."

Do it again Lord! Let your fire fall!

Come Lord Jesus Christ in All Your Might and Power and Majesty ~ Spirit of the Living God ~ fall afresh on us! Come Lord Jesus Come! "Yes I am coming soon!"

"Nothing is impossible with God." Yes I am here and I am coming soon! And I am taking care of all your needs and their needs this second ~ I'm taking care of all they lack and you lack right now." Thank you and Praise you Jesus. Amen, Amen and Amen.

I can at all times and in all situations:

"Get bitter" or "Get better" because I have His grace. JESUS is alive in me and I am alive in Him.

Praise God from Whom All Blessings Come and Come and Come!

Choose life or death each instant.

God's solution or way or man's way out or live by human standards or live by Divine standards.

Pray with JESUS and with Mary and all the angels and saints here on earth and in Heaven and you'll never pray alone. Walk with JESUS and you'll never walk alone. Suffer with JESUS and you'll never suffer alone. We are praying with JESUS. We are walking with JESUS. We are suffering with JESUS and He and Mother Mary, St. Joseph etc. are suffering with us and rejoicing with us and me in His victory.

JESUS! You are the center of everything and everyone. Father, forgive me ~ us the "root" of all my ~ our problems is that ~ me ~ myself ~ I ~ someone or something else has taken your place in my ~ our hearts ~ in my ~ our life ~ my ~ or our minds ~ spirit of self-centredness, catering to our "old nature" that JESUS nailed to the cross ~ in the Name of JESUS I cast you out ~ JESUS IS LORD AND KING!

Forgive me, my indifference towards You and others.

Forgive me, my ingratitude towards You and others.

Forgive me, my pride and spiritual blindness towards You and others.

Forgive me, my rebellion towards You and others.

Forgive me, my self-centeredness towards You and others.

Forgive me, my spirit of independence from You and from each other.

Forgive me, my lack of knowledge of You and Your Word and Promises.

Forgive me my lack of faith, hope, love and truth.

Forgive me, my spirit of division and agitation ~ my spirit of power or control over others.

Thank You, I believe I am forgiven.

WE ARE FORGIVEN IF WE ACKNOWLEDGE OUR SINS AND CHANGE BY HIS GRACE.

In the name of JESUS I bind and cast out all this junk that I have been exposed to right here and right now. Get out of my life- get out of their life! Because JESUS IS LORD ! HOW GREAT IS OUR GOD!

ALLELUIA OUR GOD REIGNS

RELAX GOD'S IN CHARGE.

But as many as received Him as Saviour, Lord, Master and King, to them He gave the power to become the Sons of God. Alleluia, We are sons of God.

How to receive Him? The Father and the Holy Spirit

~ JESUS.

By thinking about Him.

Taking Him into our minds.

Making him our fixed thought.

By studying about Him.

By living with Him.

By making Him the central fact of our lives.

Jesus, Mother Mary and Joseph I give you my heart and my soul. We give you our hearts and souls and our marriage and family and friends and church ~ our whole life and our death. Now we belong to you forever.

How? A complete spiritual surrender and commitment.

When you give yourself to Him (and to your husband)

~ He gives Himself to you and you begin to stand up straight and to believe with power.

Then you will live alive all your life; you will live alive with Faith, Hope and Love. Then you will walk with the King and be a Blessing!!

Thank you Dear Father for letting everything and everyone, especially me, be in a "humanly hopeless situation", whether we know it, admit it or not ~ so that You and You alone can show us Your Power ~ Your Love ~ Your Truth ~ Your Perfect Plan of Love and Truth ~ so that we will not be able to take the credit for something only You can do for us,

(Isaiah 48-9)

Otherwise we will only get more "puffed up" than we already are and continue to "bypass God", "rob God of His Glory."

"Our God reigns" "God Never Panics!" "He's in Charge!" because of His Name – because of His Glory and His Promises and His Love – He will come to get us out of the mess we have made of everything and everyone. O God, My God only You can do it! "Upon you my true couples I will rebuild my perfect plan for humanity and the forces of hell shall not prevail against it."

You are Peter and upon this rock I will build my church and the forces of hell shall not prevail against it. Amen.

Come Lord Jesus Come!

So be still ~ you don't have to worry, just stay in peace if you are in Christ you are a new creation!
~ Trust me no matter how bad things look Psalm 12-5
~ I know what I'm doing.
~ I am in perfect control of everyone and everything that you have confided to my care.

I am your Father and their Father, your Good Shepard and their Good Shepard, your Only Hope and their Only Hope, your Bread of Life and their Bread of Life! Just keep your eyes, you heart, your thoughts ~ everything centered on me! JESUS and JESUS and continue to love God and love others as yourself one moment at a time.

Let's continue praising and thanking the Lord for everything that is happening to us because He told us to. It may seem easier to be sad, worried, angry, lonely, or fearful but

God tells is to rejoice in Him always and to give thanks in all things. This is His Will ~ we cannot escape His Will. We may disobey it, but that won't change His Will!

He wants us to rejoice and trust Him and not to dwell on our problems ~ so that we can rejoice and be victorious over our problems and spirit of the Living God fall afresh upon me right now so that I, we and all people can continue praising the Lord all my life and in all circumstances and everywhere.

Thank You Father, Thank You Jesus. Thank You Holy Spirit. Thank You Mother Mary. Thank You all the Angels and all the Saints.

Alleluia ~ Praise the Lord!

Yesterday is gone ~ forget it. Tomorrow is not here ~ don't worry. Today is here ~ use it.

Use it to do God's will ~ use it to love God and love your neighbor as yourself. All this made possible by the gift of this new life in the Spirit ~ Praise the Lord! Who set me free to love Him and my neighbor as myself ~ Alleluia.

Don't look around.

Don't look back.

Don't look forward.

Only look up at JESUS. He can live anywhere and everywhere in victory. He has conquered sickness, the world, sin, death, sorrow, all evil and even the evil one!

Father, dear Father get us through or get us out of this mess you have allowed us to make. Thank you.

Please tell me how and where to love you and my neighbor today. Thank you Father and please live all this in me ~ otherwise it's hopeless, I can not make it.

Father keep us one, whole and well, in you so the world will know that JESUS and the HOLY SPIRIT and You are ALIVE and in Full Control Today! RELAX! God is in control! Worrying is useless and it does come from God!

Thank you my dear Mother Mary who is taking care of me and everyone.

I love you dear Mother Mary, St. Joseph and all the angels and Saints.

Thank you dear Heavenly Father.

I love you Father.

I love you Jesus.

I love you Holy Spirit.

"The problem is not to doubt or question whether our baptism, our marriage, our church, our renewals, our revivals and all the other sacraments are valid etc.

The root of all this is simple: we have listened to the "Liar" or our own "Old nature" instead of listening and obeying God and His Perfect Plan of Love and Truth which equals Justice and Peace.

Psalm 85

This sets us Free to Love God and Love our neighbor as ourselves! For the Glory of God and our good!

Come Lord JESUS! MARANATHA!

"Yes I am here and I am coming back in All MY Glory, Soon! Alleluia.

~ Our God Reigns".

~ We are waiting in Joyful hope for the full accomplishment of ALL HIS PROMISES

~ One day more to live alive in faith and one day less before Jesus returns in All His glory. One day more to live alive in joyful hope before my husband comes back.

ONE DAY AT A TIME, USA 1942 – 1946

One day at a time, with its failures and fears,
With its hurts and mistakes, its weaknesses
     and tears,
With its portion of pain and its burden of
     care,
One day at a time we must meet and must
     bear.
One day at a time to be patient and strong,
To be calm under trail and sweet under
     wrong,
Then its toiling shall pass, its sorrow shall
     cease,
It shall darken and die – the night shall bring
     peace.
One day at a time – but the day is so long,
And the heart is not brave, the soul is not
     strong.
O thou pitiful Christ be Thou near all the
     way and Mary too.

Give courage and strength for the day.

Swift cometh His answer, so clear and so
    sweet Yes, I will be with you thy trouble to
    meet. I will not forget Thee, nor fail Thee
    nor grieve, I will not forsake Thee, I never
    will leave.
Not yesterdays load we are called to bear,
Nor the morrow's uncertain and shadowy
    care,
Why should we look forward or backwards
    with dismay,
Our needs as our mercies are but for the day.
One day at a time, and the day is His day,
He has numbered its hours though they
    haste or delay,
His grace is sufficient, we walk not alone,
As the day, so the strength that He giveth
    his own.
Amen
Author Unknown

Chapter

14 *Final Words*

This is the shortest chapter of this book and perhaps the most important one! This is my biggest folly. Most people, associate marriage with their faith. My Folly has nothing to do with faith. My Folly has to do with the truth ... - ... Marriage has nothing to do with faith. Marriage has everything to do with the truth that God created marriage like he created the sun, moon, stars and animals. In the beginning of the world, God created all these things and one couple. Most people don't understand how far it goes.

The day any man or woman marries, (unless under force, like a knife to one's throat,) it is God, who says, "Yes." This is true for everyone. It is true even for those who have no religion at all and also for those who are very faithful. And even if one thinks they made a mistake, or they were too young, the truth is God will provide all his grace to make it go to the end.

I refuse to judge anybody who doesn't live like this because most people are not aware of God's fidelity to make all marriages work his way. I do not judge those who divorce. Others do not realize what is happening. They always associate marriage with feelings, faith, emotions or other ways of thinking .I do not condemn!

My best friends are all married and divorced and I get along with them very well. They say," I respect all you tell me, but do not agree!" Practically every one of them has married a second time and seem happier and more in love.

You do not need faith to stay married. Marriage is God's creation. If we try to change gravity we can't do it. But, what have we done with marriage?

We have twisted God's plan and compromise this truth in God. If you read, The Splendor of Truth by Pope John Paul the Second, he says the same thing and explains it so much better.

The word of God must come in marriage. Love without the truth or truth without love doesn't work. When love and truth meet, justice and peace kiss. Everything is in the right place. It's where God wants it to be. We cannot change God's creation.

If I say I don't like gravity and try to defy it by throwing a vase out the window it will soon smash into pieces regardless of how I feel about gravity.

It's so hard for me to see people suffer. So many marriages have problems from the beginning to the end. It is false compassion to think that we can solve divine problems by human means. Muslims have another way. Catholics have another way. Protestants have another way. The Truth is the only way!

Today, so many young people do not want to marry anymore. There is an increase in abortion and homosexuality but God will never change. Glory! Glory! Halleluiah!

God leaves us free. We can say," yes" or "no" to his plan. He will never change! I do not judge anyone. It is My Folly! I'm just waiting for others to be enlightened. I am an intercessor. Without the guidance of the Holy Spirit, I might do exactly as everyone else. My hope and prayer is that the Holy Spirit will touch them and do for them exactly what he has done for me!

It is My Folly. I even had a young priest, someone I like very much, say to me, "Oh Carmela, you go too far." He couldn't understand it! For those who believe this truth no explanation is necessary, but for those who do not believe this truth no explanation is possible.

Yes, I expect to be reunited with my husband based on God's promise: Hope against all hope! For God nothing is impossible! For God one day is like a thousand years. There is no time limit!

I am ready Lord! My room is full of stuff like heavy boots and bulky sweaters and all the things I need to go back to live with my husband in the center of France. Our patron saint is John the Baptist. Like Sir Thomas Moore, he said the truth and what happened? They had their heads chopped off!

I know most people don't agree with me. But I have the courage to live My Folly. Finally, like Thomas Moore in the movie, A Man for All Seasons, I have courage because of Truth!

I hope and pray that one day we will have the revelation and courage to campaign and march against "Divorce", similar to those of the Right to Life Movement. Abortion is horrible as it destroys human life. Divorce is also horrible because it destroys God's Perfect Plan for all humanity!

May God Bless Us.

Made in the USA
Charleston, SC
07 November 2011